Beyond the Back Yard:

Train Your Dog To Listen Anytime, Anywhere!

First Edition: 2015

Second Edition: 2016 by Fenzi Dog Sports Academy Publishing

© 2016 Denise Fenzi

All uncredited photos © 2016 Denise Fenzi

Cover Illustration by: Lili Chin | www.doggiedrawings.net

Designed by: Rebeccah Aube | www.pawsink.com
Paws & Ink! A Creative Blend of Dog Training & Graphic Design

ISBN NUMBER: 978-0-9887818-5-6

Beyond the Back Yard
Table of Contents

Acknowledgements

I know that people often say "this book wouldn't have happened if it hadn't been for…"

Well, it's true. This book really would not have happened if it hadn't been for what started out as a casual online discussion among fellow dog trainers and students of the Fenzi Dog Sports Academy. After 20 minutes of musing about what dedicated owners really want - a pet dog who is able to cooperate under distracting circumstances with a reasonable time commitment for training - it became clear that this book didn't exist. Yet! It also became clear that not only did I have the knowledge to write it, but that I had to write it, and my online friends would not take no for an answer! In fact, I had to start it RIGHT THEN so that it didn't fall by the wayside. And that is exactly what happened. I started writing and those same friends cheered me on, provided photographs to smooth my road, gave me feedback on my plan, and practiced my ideas with their own students in their own classes. So, when I say, "Thanks, it wouldn't have happened without you," I mean it. So, thank you! As a token of my appreciation, I have made the companion "Instructor Curriculum" book free for professional trainers to use in their class settings.

I also wish to thank all of my students over the years. I have learned a tremendous amount from each of you. In particular, I appreciate those of you who brought me the most challenging dogs; the ones who kept me up at night worrying and thinking about how to best communicate our need for cooperation while respecting their needs as well.

And finally, thanks as always to my editor Crystal Barrera for making sense out of my sometimes incomprehensible scribble, to Rebeccah Aube for always turning out a beautiful book for me, to Lilli Chin for designing a charming cover that portrayed exactly what I wanted to communicate, and to my family, for patiently accepting that every once in a while, I will become so consumed with my writing that I am pretty much inaccessible for days at a time. I'm back now.

About the author

Denise Fenzi is a professional dog trainer who specializes in building cooperation and extreme working precision in competitive dog sports teams. Her personal passions are Competitive Obedience and spreading high quality information about no force (motivational) dog training. In addition to travelling worldwide to teach dog training seminars, Denise writes prolifically for the Dog Sports audience, and she also runs a very successful online school for competition dog sports - the Fenzi Dog Sports Academy. You can find all of her books at www.thedogathlete.com, her school at www.fenzidogsportsacademy.com, and her blog at www.denisefenzipetdogs.com

PET DOG TRAINERS, PLEASE READ

If you run classes for pet dogs and you would like to offer distraction training classes that are highly compatible with the materials offered in this book, please visit www.thedogathlete.com Select "free downloads" from the left hand side menu, and help yourself to the Instructor Curriculum PDF that you will find there. That free e-book provides you with a six week long class, complete with a series of lesson plans and short videos to assist you in applying the concepts from this book to a group setting. You will also find additional training ideas at www.denisefenzipetdogs.com

Foreword

Once in a while, a dog training book comes along that is completely different. A book that is much more than what we expect, and we wonder why it hasn't already been written. A book that is destined to run at the head of the pack. Denise Fenzi's *Beyond the Back Yard: Train Your Dog To Listen Anytime Anywhere!* is such a book. I absolutely love it.

There is simply nothing like *Beyond the Back Yard* on the market; this book starts where most dog training books end. Rather than describing how to teach basic manners in controlled situations, *Beyond the Back Yard* assumes that your dog will usually come, sit, stay, and walk nicely on leash in non-distracting settings. It then takes a huge, quantum leap by teaching dedicated dog owners how to control their dogs when away from home, when off-leash, and when in the presence of tempting alternatives and distractions. In other words, *Beyond the Back Yard* teaches what to do in the real world and without the crutch of a cookie in hand. This, of course, is what dog owners really want to know — a training plan that works in real-life situations, when guests come to the front door, during picnics in the park, when a cat or squirrel darts across the road, and when off-leash in parks and on walks.

For many years, Denise's specialty has been training dogs and other competitors for high-level competitions in which dogs are required to work reliably and precisely under extreme distractions without the aid of leashes, halters, harnesses, or food and toys to gain cooperation and control. Denise has titled multiple dogs in multiple sports, including obedience, and she has garnered an impressive array of accolades. The hallmark of her competition dogs is engagement, happiness, willingness, pizazz, and really beautiful obedience.

I am delighted that Denise has taken the time to apply her professional experience and expertise to the training of pet dogs and their human companions. In *Beyond the Back Yard*, you'll learn how dogs learn, what they understand, and how to teach off-leash reliability, even at a distance, when distracted, and without the continued necessity of any training aid. Ultimately, your dog will be welcome in far more places as a result.

Both you and your dog are going to be happy that you have read this book.

Dr. Ian Dunbar
Founder, Association of Professional Dog Trainers

Preface
Beyond the Back Yard

**Is this book right for you? To find out,
answer the following two questions:**

Question #1:
Can your dog perform a variety of basic behaviors such as sit, come, stay, and walk nicely on a leash?

If you answered yes, that's great! You'll need those skills if you want to make use of this book, because this book is radically different from other dog training books that you might have read. You see, this book starts with the assumption that your dog is already trained to follow your basic obedience commands.

Question #2:
Can your dog perform those behaviors away from home, without a cookie in your hand, or under distraction? For example, can your dog sit, come, stay, and walk nicely on a leash in the local park? When your guests come to the door? When you pick your kids up from school? How about when a squirrel darts across the road?

Nala sits perfectly at home for a cookie!

But Nala is still learning to cooperate away from home and without a cookie nearby.

If you answered, "not so much," then this is exactly the right book for you.

The skills you have now are very important, and the fact that you have mastered them suggests that you have taken the time to become a responsible pet owner. Whether you've done this through books, classes, or trial and error, you have trained your dog to understand a variety of highly desirable basic behaviors. Congratulations!

But there is another stage of training. It is incredibly important, but unfortunately, it is not usually discussed adequately (if it's discussed at all!) in most training books or classes. This stage of training is where you take the behaviors that your dog knows and teach your dog to do them under distraction, away from home, and without a cookie in your hand.

The fact is, what a dog knows is not a yes/no proposition; it's contextual. This can be extremely frustrating! If you think about it, though, the same is true for people. What we know how to do is also contextual.

Here's an example: Your child sings all day long in your house. It's adorable, so when your family comes over for Christmas, you ask your young child to sing for your guests. Now, rather than opening up in song as she does on any other occasion, she either hides, runs off, or flat out refuses to perform. This isn't a physical problem; she still knows how to sing. Rather, your child won't sing because she is either fearful of performing publicly or she is distracted by her cousins in the other room. Both of these issues - fear and distraction - are real and well understood by parents around the world. While parents often find this frustrating or irritating, expressing your frustration to your child does nothing to change the reality; your song bird is not going to sing right now. Your child can learn to perform in public, but since this book is about dog training, not child rearing, we won't go into that here. Instead, let's talk about dogs.

You've attended several training classes. Good! You understand that giving your dog treats is a simple way to get behaviors and to communicate what you are looking for. Great! Your dog quickly learned to perform all of the basics, and even a few tricks just for fun. Even better!

Deacon learned more than obedience during his initial training; he learned a few tricks too!

But now, in spite of diligently practicing over a period of weeks or months, it seems that the only time your dog is willing to perform is when he's at home, with nothing else interesting going on, and when a cookie is being dangled temptingly close to your dog's drooling mouth. What good is all of that dog training if your dog cannot perform when you really need it? When can you expect to get some useful obedience in public?

Right now, actually. The truth is, even if you faithfully work with your dog every single day for five years, nothing is going to change if you keep practicing the way you are now. Your dog may perform faster and with more and more enthusiasm over time, but that improvement will remain limited to your kitchen, when nothing else is going on, and with a cookie in your hand. If that is all that you have taught your dog, then that is all he will know to give back in return. It's the nature of learning. Dogs do what works for them to the best of their abilities. Same as humans, really.

Agility dogs compete under challenging conditions. Handlers teach their dogs to ignore distractions, and you can too!

Have you ever watched an agility or obedience competition on TV and wondered how those handlers were able to remove their dog's leash without the dog taking off to visit all of the other dogs? Not only that, but those dogs then perform a series of obstacles at top speed, seemingly oblivious to the possibility of a reward. I can guarantee that those teams did not practice in their kitchen, day after day. I can also guarantee that the owner didn't just one day take the dog in public, remove the leash, say a quick prayer, and get the behaviors she wanted in front of the cameras.

Instead, those people trained their dogs to perform under distraction, in new environments, and without a steady stream of cookies. They didn't spend their entire lives doing it, either. Most dog sports competitors spend no more than an hour or two a week training each dog - and that is for exceptionally complicated work under challenging conditions. If all you want is a few basics like a recall, a stay, and a loose leash as you head down the street, your time commitment can be significantly less. The trick is to train smarter, not longer. If you go in with a plan, you'll find that the total number of hours spent is quite minimal indeed.

This book will give you a plan to move from the acquisition of behaviors phase - where you are right now - through the proofing and generalization phases of dog training. In more basic language, that means your dog will learn to cooperate away from home, with interesting things going on around him, and without a cookie in your hand.

If you commit to about ten minutes a day for a few months, you will see dramatic progress. As a result of that progress, you will find that your dog is welcome more places. As a result of that, your willingness and enthusiasm to take your dog more places will increase. As a result of that, you will find that people enjoy your dog's company more. And as a result of that, your choice to acquire a dog will have seemed very smart, because now you have a reliable friend with whom to share many more years.

And the final result? A deeper, richer bond with your dog. Which, one hopes, was the point of training your dog in the first place.

The author rests with her dog Raika.

A NOTE ON HOW TO USE THIS BOOK

This book has been split into three parts.

The first part is educational. It provides information about the theory and philosophy of training. This section will be valuable for everyone, but especially if you're the kind of person who likes to know why you're doing something a certain way before you do it.

The second part is practical. It's the "how-to" part of the book. Here, I will lay out the plan you'll be following to help your dog respond to your cues even when the world is exciting or you don't have cookies. If you're the kind of person who likes to jump right in, you can start here.

Finally, the third part is problem-solving. It will help you troubleshoot any issues that arise. In addition, if you find that you really enjoyed the training process, it will guide you in finding more opportunities for working with your dog.

Now, pick a part, and get started!

Part One:
Educational

,

Chapter 1
How Dogs Learn

While dog training does not require a degree in animal behavior, it is useful to understand how dogs learn. Although you could just follow the lesson plan presented in Part 2 of this book and be successful, it's helpful to know WHY the lessons are set up as they are. Plus, if you understand how your dog learns, you will be able to teach her more than what's presented in this book. You'll also be better able to solve problems that arise.

All animals, including humans, will maximize their well-being in the process of learning - which is just a fancy way of saying that animals do what works best for them. This includes getting things like food or desired objects as well as a sense of emotional well-being, such as feeling safe, happy, or engaged. Animals avoid things that make them uncomfortable and seek out things that they like, want, or need. So if you want an animal to do something for you (called a behavior), then either provide a pleasant consequence when she cooperates, or an unpleasant consequence when she doesn't.

Sometimes an animal is consciously thinking about what is happening around her. At other times, she is learning without any thought at all. In both cases, the animal is learning. Let's take a moment to look at each of these scenarios, because they are important to understand.

When your dog is making choices and is aware of what she is learning, you are using operant conditioning. Although you probably didn't realize it at the time, you were using operant conditioning when you taught your dog to perform some basic behaviors. Operant conditioning simply means that your dog makes an association between doing something and the resulting consequence. Nothing more, nothing less.

There are 3 basic ways you can use operant conditioning:

1. Your dog learns that when she does something you want, something awesome happens. For example, you may have taught your dog to sit by using a cookie.

2. Your dog learns that if she doesn't do what you want, something unpleasant happens. Some people teach their dogs to sit by pulling up on the collar.

3. Your dog learns through a combination of each of the above. Cookies when she sits, and receiving a collar correction when she doesn't.

Each time you give your dog a cue or command to do something, she makes a choice. She can calculate the sum of the possible motivators with the possible punishers and choose whether or not to comply. If complying with you works in her favor, she'll likely obey. Same as with people.

There's another form of learning, and this one is a bit more subtle. It's called classical conditioning. Unlike operant conditioning, where the animal is making choices, classical conditioning doesn't require any conscious effort at all to learn. It just happens.

Animals are learning all the time, whether we are aware of it or not. When you were teaching your dog to sit - no matter how you did it - she was learning more than just how to sit. She was learning about training in general; is it fun and something to look forward to, or something unpleasant and best avoided? She learned how much she enjoys (or doesn't enjoy) your company. She learned if the world is a safe, predictable place, or if it's unsafe and anxiety-provoking.

Operant conditioning is being used to teach this puppy to stay on his mat. At the same time, classical conditioning is always at work!

As you may have already guessed, people have the same experiences with classical conditioning. If you've ever had a really super teacher who was patient, kind, and consistent, yet held you to high expectations, you know how hard you worked to learn and to please her, and how much you wanted to be in her company.

On the other hand, if you've ever had a teacher or an employer who was grumpy, demanding, unreasonable, or unpredictable, you know how anxious you felt in her presence. You may have even discovered that under her supervision, you were unable to do even simple tasks because your nervousness blocked your ability to learn or to perform correctly. That is because fear overwhelms rational thought. Again, this is true in all animals, including dogs and humans.

Since classical conditioning isn't conscious, you might find yourself feeling anxiety and unpleasantness well after the event that caused those reactions in the first place. Many parents who did not enjoy their school years have reported feeling upset or anxious when they first walked into their child's school classroom, even twenty years later! Long after they have forgotten exactly what it was about school that was unpleasant, they still harbor the negative feelings. That's classical conditioning at work.

Just as the dog was learning without realizing it, it is quite likely that you were teaching these lessons without realizing it either. It is critically important for your dog to learn that training time is pleasant because fear and anxiety block effective and efficient learning. The more your dog is able to relax and look forward to her lessons, the more quickly she will master them and work to please you. If you want your dog to be an engaged learner, then make it a priority to set up training sessions that are short, positive, and rewarding for your dog. If you express disappointment in her work or use physical manipulation to get the desired responses, you'll erode your working relationship by creating unpleasant classically conditioned responses to training.

These dogs appear relaxed and comfortable in their training class.

This book will use positive training methods for several reasons:

1. We want to condition our dogs to enjoy working with us so that they can learn more quickly.

2. We want our dogs to respond even when they are out of our physical reach. Dogs are smart. If compliance is gained primarily through methods that involve corrections, they quickly learn when you can and cannot enforce your commands. If your dog only complies when he is on a leash or when he is wearing a special collar, you need to consider how this relates to your training goals. How often do you need a recall on a six foot leash? Probably never; he's already with you! All dogs can figure out if they are wearing a leash, but it's a rare dog who knows if you have access to a cookie. (Note that I said "access to." Most dogs know if you have a cookie in your hand or pocket. More on this later.)

3. While residual fear and the generally easygoing nature of dogs might allow for cooperation even when enforcement is not possible, it's not much fun to have a dog cooperate because she is afraid of you. The purpose of having a dog is to enjoy the mutually beneficial relationship that can exist across species. Why create a relationship based on fear when it's not necessary?

The training plan in this book will take both operant conditioning and classical conditioning into account. You and your dog should both enjoy the process! If you aren't both having fun, go back and look at why this might be. What are you teaching your dog without meaning to? Are you doing something to scare her, even if you don't mean to? Find ways to make the process enjoyable for you both!

Chapter Two
What Motivates Your Dog?

Nikki and Bella are motivated by playing in the water.
What motivates your dog?

So now that you have a sense of how dogs learn, and why keeping your dog engaged, happy, and without fear is important to the process, let's take a look at our toolbox.

Because we want our dogs to love their training time, we have to use the right tools that will encourage them to cooperate. These tools are called "rewards," "motivators," or "reinforcers." Going forward, we'll use those terms interchangeably.

For something to be a motivator, your dog must want it. If your dog will not work for a piece of kibble, find something else. You are wasting your time using something that does not motivate your dog. The fact that your neighbor's Labrador will work for a piece of kibble has nothing to do with your dog. Find a motivator that YOUR dog truly wants and will work to earn.

So what does your dog find motivating? Rank each of the following possibilities on a scale of 1 to 10. Feel free to add your own - the more options you have, the better!

- Petting
- Praise
- Dry dog biscuits
- Cooked chicken
- Hot dogs
- A piece of pasta
- Moist store bought treats
- Kibble in a bowl
- Kibble handed over one at at time
- Fetching balls
- Playing tug
- Freedom to go outside
- Freedom to chase squirrels
- Going for a swim
- A trip to the dog park
- A walk on a trail

Most dogs find food very motivating!

Anything that your dog wants can be used as a motivator. Stella will happily work for a thrown stick picked up on the trail.

If you're not sure how two options might rank, offer them to your dog side by side, and see how he responds. If your dog has a choice between a piece of kibble or playing ball, which would he rather have? How about between a piece of cheese and a slice of hot dog? Because dogs are individuals, they each have their own personal preference. You need to identify your dog's favorite things - in some cases, the results might not be what you'd expect!

There are many types of distractions in the world.

If your dog has a lot of 8s, 9s, and 10s, then you are very fortunate. The more motivators that you can identify for your dog, the better! If your dog has few powerful motivators, then you'll need to be especially careful to set up training scenarios where your dog will end up successful.

Some of these reinforcers may have confused you. How can going for a swim or running in the dog park be used as a motivator? We'll talk about this special category of motivators in depth later on. For now, the important thing to understand is that behaviors CAN be used to motivate other behaviors. What's more, these are often our strongest motivators of all.

Be aware that the value of a motivator is contextual, so a motivator that works in one environment might not work in another. Kibble might be an 8 in your kitchen but only a 3 in your backyard. That's because distractions also have a value, and on any given occasion, your dog may also be considering the alternatives. If chasing a squirrel is more valuable than your cookie, then chasing the squirrel wins. Indeed, as we start this process, you might find that some distractions are more powerful than anything that you might have to offer! That's completely normal. Time, consistency, patience, and a few tricks of the trade will carry the day. Settle in and we'll get there.

This brings us to our second list. Now it's time to take a look at the distractions that are giving you grief. Take a look at this list and consider the ones that you would like to work on - even if they seem less interesting to your dog. You will need both easy and challenging distractions on your list in order to use this book. Here are some possibilities to get you started; note that anything on your motivator list is very likely to also show up on this list as a distraction.

- A slice of bread out of reach on the countertop
- A slice of meat out of reach on the countertop
- A piece of pasta on a chair, at eye level, in a container
- A piece of pasta on the floor, accessible
- A family member sitting in a chair
- A family member walking through the house
- A family member talking excitedly
- A stranger sitting in a chair
- A stranger walking through the house
- A stranger ringing your doorbell
- Another dog on a sit stay
- Another dog walking by on a leash
- Another dog running in the dog park
- A squirrel sitting in a tree
- A squirrel running to a tree

This list can be grouped into four basic categories: being in the presence of food, around strangers, outside of the house, and near other dogs. Within those categories, your dog might find some possibilities extremely distracting and others almost neutral. It's fine to say that other dogs are a distraction, but at what level? To train for distractions, it is critical that we be able to identify both lower and higher levels of distraction for the same category. A dog sitting quietly with his owners will rarely be the same amount of distraction as a dog running full speed across the dog park. If you don't spend time differentiating these possibilities, you will struggle to set your training sessions up for success.

Before we move on, there's one last thing that we need to talk about: what to do when your dog gets it wrong. The truth is, sometimes your dog will fail to do what you want even if he wanted the available motivator. But how can we keep training fun and enjoyable without correcting our dogs when they are wrong?

It's actually pretty easy. We'll simply mark failure by taking away something the dog wanted. Instead of getting a cookie for cooperating, we'll take that cookie away as a consequence for failing to perform.

Since humans are also subject to the laws of learning, here is a human example to explain how it works. Let's pretend that you're a contestant on a game show. There is a huge stack of cash laid out in front of you, just out of reach. If you answer a question correctly, the host will give you $5,000! But if you answer the question incorrectly, he'll take that money away from you. Because you want to avoid this very unpleasant consequence, you will work hard to get the answers right - and the host has your cooperation without forcing you to do it.

It works the same way with our dogs. Let's say you asked your dog to sit in the kitchen for the piece of cookie that you are holding. Instead of cooperating, your dog chooses to go and sniff the counter where the rest of the cookies are located - he's hoping for the whole stash! Your response is to return the cookie to the cookie jar. Your dog did not get the big pile of cookies, and worse yet, he didn't get the one you were offering, either.

Part of excellent training is teaching your dog that a bird in the hand is worth two in the bush. Or maybe we should say, a cookie in the hand is worth two in the mouth! Yes, dogs do figure this out. Competition dog trainers do it all the time, and your dog can learn this lesson as well.

Of course, the goal of this book is to gain compliance under a wide range of training scenarios, not competition obedience, so here is an example that doesn't use a cookie. Let's say your dog wants to go outside. The opportunity to go outside is the reinforcer in this case. You ask your dog to sit and politely wait at the door. If he fails, you respond by closing the door, which means that your dog has just lost access to the motivator - the great outdoors! Since that is not quite the reaction your dog was expecting or hoping for, you will likely see your dog's willingness to wait politely at the door improve the next time he finds himself in a similar predicament.

Taking away something that a dog was hoping to get is a very powerful form of communication, but it must be used with caution. Dogs, like people, thrive on success. Too many failures in a row and you'll find that your dog walks away from training altogether - just like you would give up on the game show if all that happened was the host taking the money away.

To avoid this, you need to set your dog up for success. He should win about 80% of the time. So how do you do this? The next chapter will look carefully at why dogs do or do not perform correctly under a variety of circumstances.

Dean has learned that if he jumps out of the car without a release, he will be put back and the hatch will be closed. His freedom will be taken away.

Dogs thrive on success.
Set up challenges where your dog can win most of the time!

Chapter Three
What Does Your Dog Know?

Robin "knows" how to sit and stay, even away from home and on a pile of rocks!

This book assumes that your dog already knows how to perform your target behaviors (also called base behaviors). What I haven't told you yet is that what a dog knows is actually contextual. In other words, your dog probably doesn't know what you think she does unless you've done specific training. That specific training, called generalization, is the process of applying information from one context to another. It's very important to do this because dogs are notoriously poor at generalization.

Does your dog know how to sit on command? Let's find out!

Go to your dog's most familiar training area and grab a pile of delicious cookies. Make sure she knows you have them and that she is eager to earn them. Now face your dog and ask her to sit. Your dog should enthusiastically put her rear end on the ground. Excellent!

Let's try it again, except with a small change. This time, turn your back on your dog so that you are facing the wall. Ask her to sit.

What happened?

I'm willing to bet that she failed to perform. Not because she was unmotivated or fearful. Not because she was distracted or in a new place. And not because she couldn't hear you. I know all this because the only thing you changed was the direction that you were facing; the first time you were facing your dog and the second time you turned your back on your dog. So what went wrong?

Your dog failed to perform because you changed the context. She learned to sit with you facing her, and now you've changed the picture! Your dog isn't stubborn or bad. Your dog simply has not learned which variables are - or are not - relevant. To be blunt, she doesn't know "sit." Instead, she knows "owner standing in front of me in the kitchen holding a cookie in front of my nose and saying the word sit."

But what if you tried this test and your dog passed? That's great! She has started to learn sit. Let's see just how well she's learned it. Take your dog to a familiar place and have an obvious motivator in your hand. We want your dog trying her hardest so we can safely conclude that any failure to perform is due to holes in your basic training as opposed to a lack of motivation.

- Can your dog sit when you are sitting in a chair?
- Can your dog sit when you lying on the floor?
- Can your dog sit when you are staring at the ceiling?
- Can your dog sit when you are behind the door?

Come up with as many variations as possible - within reason. The goal is not to cause your dog to fail; the goal is to find the weaknesses in your basic training so that you can work through them. As you do this, be sure to maintain sympathy for your dog. She's trying, so your job is to provide measured challenges so that she can succeed.

For those attempts where your dog failed, ask yourself if there is a way that you could make it easier. For example, if your dog cannot sit when you are in a chair, how about if you simply lean on that chair? Reward generously for success, and stay positive in the face of failure - simply try again with an easier variation. Don't forget to end each successful repetition with a tasty cookie and a verbal release, so your dog knows that it's okay to get up.

Will your dog stay if you are sitting in a chair?
How about if you are away from home?

Now let's consider how the above exercise relates very directly to the point of this book.

Can your dog sit when there is no cookie in your hand? (reducing reinforcers)

Can your dog sit when there is a bowl of food sitting on the counter? (distraction)

Can your dog sit in a brand new location? (environmental change)

Can your dog sit when there is a strange person in the room? (fear)

As you look over ALL of these possibilities, it is important to understand that failure to perform has nothing to do with being stubborn, stupid, or manipulative. If your dog knew how to sit in that exact circumstance, then she would do it! She wants that cookie and she can easily get it if she cooperates with you! Failure is simply a lack of understanding.

If she fails to perform because you are not holding a cookie, then she does not understand that you have access to the location where the cookies are stored - and she needs your help to get to them.

35

This German Shepherd can sit easily!

Until....a person walks by with a favorite toy.

If she fails to perform when there is a bowl of food on the counter, then she does not understand that she cannot access the food that is there unless you choose to give it to her.

If she fails to sit politely before you open the gate to the dog park, then she does not understand that you will not open that gate until she offers to sit and wait.

If she fails to sit in a new location, then she does not understand that sitting in a new location will be rewarded, and that you hold onto those cookies until the two of you work out the details.

If she fails to perform when there is a strange person in the room, she does not understand that she is safe. Until she believes in her well-being, the cookie will not operate as a motivator.

In short, if your dog does not perform under any of these circumstances, it is because she has not yet learned how to do so.

She needs to learn! And you can teach her! But more practice in your kitchen with a handful of cookies won't do anything to further your dog's ability to perform correctly under a wide range of circumstances. You need to systematically train your dog to perform in each context.

Indeed, the process of generalization is where competition dog trainers, who perform at crowded dog shows under stressful conditions, spend the vast majority of their training time. Competition people are fond of saying that teaching the behaviors is the easy part. But getting those behaviors to hold up under adversity? That is the challenge.

And it's why you are here!

Because Dazzle is obedient in public, he is a welcome companion at public events.

Chapter Four
Changing The Challenge

Pira is practicing a one minute stay in the kitchen. He has "met" criteria if he holds that stay for a full minute.

To help dogs learn to generalize their behaviors, we have to know when to increase the challenge level. This is something dog trainers call "raising criteria."

Before we can raise criteria, though, your dog needs to meet criteria. Basically, this means that your dog needs to successfully complete the behavior to your specifications. For example, if your goal is a 30 second sit stay under mild distraction and your dog performs a sit stay for 30 seconds with a piece of bread sitting on the counter, then your dog has met criteria. But what if your dog goes to the counter and sniffs for the scent of the bread instead of performing the stay? Then we would say that your dog has not met criteria.

When your dog meets criteria you'll reward him with a motivator, but when he fails to succeed, you'll withhold that motivator. (You'll also make sure that he is unable to get the bread on the counter, since helping himself to the distraction would have been very reinforcing - but not reinforcing what you wanted!)

When your dog consistently meets criteria by ignoring the bread on the counter and performing correctly, you can raise criteria. This simply means you'll ask your dog to do more in order to earn a cookie. But… what is "more"? And how many successes do we want to see before we raise criteria again?

Now Pira is asked to stay in the living room while his owner watches from another room. Criteria has been raised!

When it's time to raise criteria, the trick is to select a new challenge that your dog is likely to meet. If you work to raise criteria in a systematic and measured fashion, you will find that your dog makes progress extremely quickly while maintaining a positive attitude throughout his training sessions. It's good to ask more of your dog, because it keeps him thinking and working for you, but if you ask for too much all at once, you'll demoralize him with excessive failure. At the same time, if you raise criteria too slowly, your dog will become bored and his progress will slow down. In other words, raising criteria is something of a Goldilocks question: how much is just right?

There are no hard and fast rules about raising (or lowering) criteria, but there are certainly some general principles:

- If you ask your dog to perform the same behavior in the same basic set up five times in a row, and he is successful at least four of those times, it's time to raise criteria. Make it harder!

- If your dog fails more than half of the repetitions, then you need to lower criteria. You asked for too much so you need to make it easier in order to keep your dog in the game.

- And if your dog is right in the middle, or if you're in doubt about whether or not to change the current challenge level, then you should stick with the current criteria. Practicing a few extra repetitions of success won't do any harm at all. In fact, it might even do wonders for a nervous or insecure dog.

Dogs often let us know with their body language if we're moving too quickly. If your dog shows signs of distress while training, then it's time to lower criteria. Or better yet, end that session and try again later with a lower level of challenge.

Here are some signs that your dog is stressed:

- Randomly sniffing the ground, even if there's nothing there.

- Lowered ears.

- Avoiding eye contact with you.

- Licking his lips.

- Leaving the training session.

- An overall demeanor that suggests he would rather not be training anymore.

Hiding behind his owner.

Head low with a roached back.

Ears back and eyes partially closed.

Ears back.

Lip licking.

But HOW do you raise or lower criteria? What are the relevant factors? There are three primary ways to change the challenge level: intensity, proximity, and duration. Each one of these factors will influence your ability to get the behavior when the circumstances have changed. Let's look at each one in turn.

Intensity

Intensity is a function of how much the circumstance has changed from the dog's point of view. For example, moving a training session from your kitchen to your bedroom is a change, but it is not as intense of a change as moving to a public park. When your dog is failing to respond well in a new place, consider your options for reducing the intensity to allow your dog a better chance at success.

It is critical that you set up the environment so your dog can be successful.

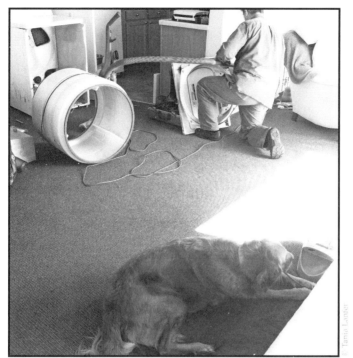

Pira is now practicing his down stay under increased intensity; there is a stranger fixing an appliance in the same room!

Instead of moving from the kitchen to the park, how about moving to the backyard, followed by the front yard, followed by in front of your neighbor's house? A slow and steady progression, marked with tons of success, breeds confidence and enthusiasm in your working partner. These are very desirable qualities in any student, canine or otherwise!

When talking about specific distractions, intensity refers to the amount of change in the distraction itself. A steaming roast on your countertop will be a much more intense distraction for your dog than a steaming plate of broccoli.

The intensity of the distraction will be relative to what you are offering. If your dog is interested in a slice of bread on the counter but you have a hot dog in your pocket as a motivator, then you are likely to "win" when the dog compares the alternatives. That is not to say that your dog won't be distracted by the piece of bread, but the odds of his being able to work through his distraction successfully are much higher if what you have to offer is better than the alternative. We'll use this to our advantage over the course of our training.

Proximity

Proximity is another word for distance. In dog training, we use the word in relation to two possibilities. One is how close the dog is to the distraction; being close to a distraction generally increases its attractiveness, thus increasing the likelihood that your dog will fail to meet criteria. The other consideration is proximity between the dog and handler. Being close to the handler tends to increase success. When you are close to your dog, he is reminded of both his relationship to you and of the treats that you have. When working with distractions, ask yourself if you are appropriately placed in relation to the location of the distraction.

Pira practices a down stay with students in the distance.

When you are working on generalizing your training to new locations, you might head to a public park. If you select a park that has off-leash dogs running and playing, consider whether you should be close or far from the distraction. What distance is your dog ready for? When you are looking for ways to make your dog more successful, consider your proximity to various challenges and make changes gradually.

Now Pira practices the same behavior with the students much closer.

Duration

Duration refers to how long your dog must work to earn a motivator. A sit cue is generally easier for a dog to perform than loose leash walking because it can be performed quickly and then rewarded, while loose leash walking is a behavior that the dog must maintain for a period of time before receiving any reinforcement.

When extending the duration of behaviors, whether a sit stay at your front door or walking politely down the street with a loose leash, consider making the overall picture easier. For example, when adding duration, you want to reduce the intensity of the environment or the

Dazzle will be expected to hold his down stay until lunch is finished. Dazzle must understand the criteria of duration (all of lunch!) and the criteria of proximity (food!)

proximity to additional challenges. Try a sit command when your dog is thinking about a loose dog in the distance rather than loose leash walking as you head straight towards the dog.

But let's say you really want to work on your loose leash walking! Fine - focus on it! Master it in your house with no distractions first! When that looks good for longer stretches of time between reinforcers, you can head out into public. But this time, go for five seconds of loose leash walking instead of two minutes, because five seconds might be more than enough under this new scenario. Doing this combines the issue of distraction with the issue of duration in order to create a situation in which your dog can succeed.

How about working on your stay cue? Start in your house in a quiet space. That way you can increase the time (duration), decrease the intensity (no distractions), and stay nearby (increased proximity). Now add a tiny distraction by walking around or moving in and out of sight. Walk towards the front door. Open the door. Ring the doorbell. Do not progress from one step until the prior step has been mastered. And whenever you raise your criteria (for example, from opening the door to ringing the doorbell), remember to scale back on duration! A five second sit when the doorbell rings is surely as impressive as a two minute sit with absolutely nothing happening. In this example, you have raised criteria by asking your dog to perform under significant

*Make sure you have a range of options when starting
your distraction training.*

intensity, but you did it in a way that set him up for success by asking him to do it for a shorter period of time. Your dog became stronger, so next time you might be looking at 7 seconds. Another win/win for you and your dog!

Remember that slice of bread sitting on the counter that we described earlier? How could we raise criteria there?

As always, you have options. Try a piece of cheese instead of a piece of bread - that's more intense for your dog. But keep it on the counter and stand in the same spot so that the intensity increases but the proximity and duration do not.

Or... place that piece of bread on the chair near your dog - the bread is the same, but the proximity to the distraction just increased without any change in either duration or intensity.

Or... keep the same piece of bread at the same height on the countertop, but instead of asking your dog to perform a ten second sit stay, shoot for twenty seconds. Now you've increased duration without changing proximity or intensity.

Any of these options are reasonable, and the more you cycle through them, the better! Like people, dogs get bored with the same old games. So in one session, why not cycle through all of those possibilities? It will only take a few minutes, and when the session is over, your dog will have a better understanding of the behavior. Stay means stay, even with varying levels of intensity, proximity, or duration. Good dog! Better yet, because your dog's understanding of what stay means improved, you'll be ready to increase the intensity of that distraction AND make it closer it to the dog. You're making progress!

And if your dog is unsuccessful? I'll provide a much more detailed answer later in this book, but for now, the simple answer is to lower criteria - but do not go all the way back to the last successful step. Find something in between! So instead of scaling up to cheese or back down to a slice of bread, maybe a reasonable middle step would be a piece of bread with butter on it. As soon as your dog shows the ability to manage the bread and butter, try the cheese again. Your dog needs to be exposed to challenges, so don't be afraid to try them!

The factors of proximity, intensity, and duration all work together, and all three should be considered when you are raising criteria within your work. Each factor - proximity, intensity, and duration - creates its own types of challenges and needs to be planned for accordingly!

As you read this, you might be overwhelmed by all of the possibilities. Rather than becoming paralyzed with fear, simply ask yourself, "What is just a little more impressive?" or "What is a little less impressive?" Your goal is to create a dog who is slightly more impressive every day. If it helps, you can keep a calendar with your crowning achievements for each week! As you look back, week by week, you'll be amazed at what you're accomplishing.

Now that you know how generalization can influence your dog's ability to understand what you're asking, how to raise criteria, and how the factors of intensity, proximity, and duration can be modified to set your dog up for success, you can create training challenges that are attainable. This will build confidence in your canine student and lead both of you on the path to success.

These three dogs are succeeding with challenges of intensity (popular treat), proximity (right under their noses) and duration (while owner takes a photo!)

The plan that is laid out in the second part of this book will address the variables of intensity, proximity, and duration in relation to a food based distraction, but there are more things out there that your dog is likely to be distracted by. After you get to the point where you have completed the food distraction chapter and you have taken that training on the road to lots of new locations, you'll want to come back to this chapter to create a plan for the other types of distractions that you will encounter in life. The concepts of proximity, intensity, and duration will help you when you are working with your dog on his other interests, like greeting people or playing with toys that may not belong to him!

Before we get to work, though, we need to look at one more consideration.

Chapter Five
Understanding Distractions

Before we wrap up Part 1, let's talk more about distractions. Introducing distractions will be a big component to the lesson plan I will lay out in Part 2. This needs to be done thoughtfully, otherwise you're pretty much guaranteeing that your dog will snatch your distraction and will forget the point of your training. Understanding distractions will make it much easier to set your dog up for success.

Let's start by differentiating controlled distractions from uncontrolled ones. A controlled distraction is anything that you can prevent your dog from enjoying, either partially or completely. For example, visiting with another dog who is on a leash is controlled, because you can keep your dog out of range of the visitor. Squeaky toys can be held out of reach, and food can be placed in containers.

An uncontrolled distraction, on the other hand, is any distraction that you have no ability to control. These often give you grief and make your training much harder. Off-leash dogs are generally an uncontrolled distraction because they can approach you and there is no way to stop them. Squirrels, deer, and other wildlife are also uncontrolled; as much as you might want to ask these critters to stop running and being so attractive to your dog, you'll have little luck getting your way.

Luckily, other than off-leash dogs and wildlife, most distractions are indeed controllable when the situation is set up for training purposes. Let's look at this a bit closer.

If you take a slice of bread and place it in a container, you control that distraction. Your dog can visit the bread. Your dog can admire the bread and stare longingly at it,

This lunchmeat is controlled because it is in a baggie.

but your dog does not have thumbs, so she cannot actually get to the bread. Even if she knocks the container off the counter, you can pick it up long before she can chew it open. In this case, the distraction is controlled by your ability to restrict access.

This lunchmeat is controlled for dogs that cannot reach the top of the table, but possibly uncontrolled for others.

Another example of controlled access takes place anytime there is a fence between the dog and whatever she might want. Examples include a swimming pool that is fenced (for a dog who enjoys swimming), another dog behind a fence (for a dog who wishes to visit), or even a bowl of food that has been placed behind a fence (for a dog who

*This lunchmeat is controlled because an assistant is available
to prevent access by the dog.*

wants a snack, which covers most of them!). The dog may be able to see what she wants, but she cannot get to it.

You also have the option of placing an open (and accessible) motivator where your dog can get to it, but use a helper to prevent access to the distraction. By using a second person, your dog learns that you still control access to distractions, even when you are not close to those distractions. Dogs can quickly learn that humans cooperate with each other, and soon any human near any distraction reminds the dog that she cannot access that option.

Another way to use controlled distractions is by controlling the dog rather than the distraction. A classic example of controlling the dog is with a leash! With a leash, you can prevent your dog from getting to whatever might interest her. She can lunge, whine, bark, and misbehave in a variety of ways, but she still cannot access whatever it is that she wants.

Of those options for controlling distractions, controlling the dog is by far and away the least desirable for two reasons. First, we eventually want off-leash control, and a dog who is aware that leash tension is the reason she cannot get to what she wants will also be acutely aware of when the leash is removed. As soon as that happens, many dogs go full speed toward what they want. The second disadvantage of the

53

Another way to control a distraction is by controlling the dog. Use a leash! This requires a dog who enjoys other motivators more than he likes food, which may or may not apply to your dog.

leash is that the dog is not learning that she can control herself from the inside. Self control is achieved through practice and by the dog realizing that she can, indeed, make choices when something exists in the environment that she would like to have. When we hold a dog back through physical means, we are eroding the dog's internal control over her behavior.

While a leash has its place in preventing disaster as your dog develops her skills, be aware that anytime the leash tightens, you have been given a reminder that your dog is not yet ready for off-leash work. Going forward, ask yourself what you can do to change your training set ups to get a better response without any leash tension. Maybe your dog needs to be farther away, or the value of the distraction needs to be lowered.

In addition to total control, some motivators give us the option of partial control. Let's use a beloved tennis ball as an example. Let's say you place your dog on a sit stay next to a chair, then place your dog's favorite fetching ball on that chair. Instead of holding a stay, the dog gets up and grabs the ball. The dog has failed because she has not held her stay, and she's also gained satisfaction in picking up the toy. But the primary value of the ball is not in your dog's ability to pick up the ball - it's in your willingness to throw it for her! When the dog brings you the ball, instead of throwing it, you return it to the chair for another attempt at a sit stay - and your dog learns a valuable lesson. Gaining access to a motivator that requires an interactive action with a human isn't valuable if the human won't play with it.

Accidents will happen as you progress through your training. That's okay!

In many ways, this is the ideal type of training scenario because the dog figures out extremely quickly that cooperation with the human is the best option. This requires a dog who finds something more valuable than food, which you may or may not have. We will investigate this option more thoroughly in the chapter on real life distractions and motivators. In the meantime, manage your dog in the presence of uncontrolled distractions. Keep her on leash, minimize access whenever possible, and accept that life happens. Just work towards your goals and one day your dog will be trained instead of managed!

Now, let's get started with training your dog.

Part Two:
Practical Matters

Notes

Chapter 6
Introducing Distractions

It's time to take your great-at-home behaviors out into the real world. To do this, we're going to start by introducing distractions to your dog.

Remember, this book is not about teaching basic behaviors, so if you can't get your dog to sit, stay, come, or walk nicely on a leash when conditions are ideal, find a trainer, book, or internet article about teaching these behaviors using positive reinforcement techniques. THEN pick up this book.

Not sure if a trained behavior is ready for distraction training? Take this simple test:

Take your dog to your most familiar training area. With food in hand, ask your dog to perform the behavior. Your dog should respond promptly on the first or second request. If so, great! You're ready to get started.

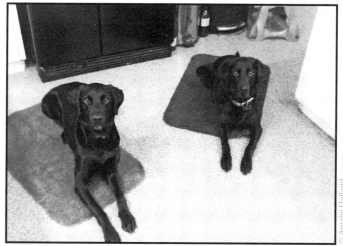

Make sure that the behaviors you ask for in distraction training are very easy for your dog.

However, if your dog wandered around first or needed many cues, you do not have a distraction problem - you have a basic training problem.

Go back and retrain that behavior. Do not use a behavior in distraction training if your dog cannot perform it easily and reliably under pristine conditions and while you're holding a cookie.

Take this test for each behavior that you would like to use in your distraction training. You can test all of your dog's behaviors now, or you can test each behavior as you need it.

Now that you know which behaviors you're going to use, it's time to choose a suitable distraction. So, what makes a distraction suitable for training? Well, it depends on the dog, but at root, it is something (anything!) that distracts your dog from performing for you and that you can control access to.

Examples of common distractions might include the following:

- Low-level distraction: Familiar person walking by, crumbs on the counter, a familiar dog in the room, or mild movement outside the window.
- Mid-level distraction: Attractive food on the counter out of reach, familiar dog or person moving quickly through your training area, or someone outside walking by your window.
- High-level distraction: Squirrel running through the trees, large amounts of steaming meat on the counter, any food on the ground, or a strange person entering the training area.

Obviously, these are very broad generalizations. In reality, what a dog finds distracting is totally dependent on the individual dog. Some dogs might find another dog playing ball nearby to be totally riveting while other dogs could not care less about the ball - or about the other dog.

As a result, it's up to you to figure out what your particular dog finds distracting. Indeed, during the process of working through this book, you will probably find distractions that you didn't realize are important to your dog. On the flip side, you might also discover that distractions you were worried about are actually of no great consequence to your dog.

These dogs work easily in the presence of other dogs. How about your dog?

Before you start the lessons, pick two things that you think your dog will find interesting, but that are relatively low value. One should be slightly higher value than the other. For example, a slice of bread on your counter might be a perfect first distraction. The second piece of food will be used to reward your dog when he cooperates, so it should be something your dog likes more than bread.

Once you've chosen both a distraction and a reward, flip to the next chapter and start working through the lesson plan. Most dogs will work through the lesson plan in about three weeks. If you work 10 minutes a day, your total investment will be about 3.5 hours. Not too bad!

Chapter 7
The Lesson Plan

In each of the following chapters, you will be working through the lessons presented here. These lessons will systematically help you introduce your dog to working through distractions, while each chapter will help you introduce new elements to your training. Once you complete all of the chapters in Part 2, you should have a very well-trained dog! If you're still struggling, or if you want a new challenge, Part 3 will help guide you.

Unless otherwise directed, you should follow these general guidelines for each lesson:

When your dog is successful, reward your dog with the "two-treat method":

- Have two cookies in your hand.
- Give your dog one cookie from your hand while you praise enthusiastically.
- Back up so that you end up farther away from the distraction, so that your dog is likely to turn back to you instead of heading to the distraction.
- Give her a second cookie when she is back with you again.

What a deal!

- Your reward should alway be higher value than your distraction.

Brito gets his cookie for ignoring the treats in the bowl on the chair

Brito gets a second cookie after backing away!

Don't worry if your dog fails. Failure is a natural part of learning. Remain calm and resist the urge to yell "no" or physically move your dog around. Instead, follow this procedure:

- Go to the distraction. Pick it up. Talk to your dog about it. Admire it together.

- And then put it back.

- Go to the same place you were before and ask the dog for the behavior again.

- If your dog fails again, make the task just a bit easier.

- For example, you might stand closer to your dog, or move the distraction a bit farther away. Or if you asked for a stay, you might change your duration from five seconds to three seconds.

Brito stares at the distraction.

Denise is ready to pick it up just in case he jumps for it!

Denise and Brito admire the treats together, but he does not get a cookie.

Brito tries again and performs correctly!

*Brito gets his two cookies and plenty
of praise too!*

**If your dog fails three times in a row, stop. The task is too hard for
your dog. Go back to the previous step or find a way to make it easier
for your dog. Ask yourself the following questions:**

- Did you use a low enough value of distraction?

- Are you using a higher value reward?

- Does your dog KNOW that you have a higher value reward?

- And this is the big one: are you SURE that your dog knows
  the base behavior in that environment when no distraction is
  present? If your dog does not know the command, you can
  repeat it till the cows come home, but you will not achieve
  success.

Each training session should be 5 minutes long OR LESS. Training
should be fun, so don't keep going unless both you and your dog are
enjoying it. You can repeat a lesson up to (but no more than) three times
in a day. Ten minutes a day is an excellent target.

Each training session should focus on one behavior only. If you'd like
to work on another behavior, do so in separate training sessions.
Each lesson should be repeated until your dog is successful at least 80%

of the time. In addition, your dog should be bright and eager to train. If she's not having fun, that training session has not been successful, no matter how well she performed!

If your dog continues to fail, make it easier! Here, the distraction is on the table rather than on the chair. Brito succeeds easily.

Lesson #1: Easy Distraction, Easy Behavior

Use a low-value distraction for this lesson!

Procedure:

1. Bring your dog into the training area.

2. While your dog is watching, place the distraction out of your dog's reach, but where she can see it. Your dog should be well aware of the distraction, so do not try to hide it!

3. Hold two cookies in your hand; you'll need them in a moment.

4. Standing close to your dog, cue a behavior she knows like a sit.

5. If your dog responds correctly, reward your dog with the two-treat method.

6. If your dog fails, admire the distraction together, then try again.

7. Repeat no more than 10 times or 5 minutes, whichever is greater.

Denise shows Brito the low value distraction.

Denise asks for a sit.

Brito sits. He gets his first cookie!

Brito gets his second cookie as he backs away.

Lesson #2: Easy Distraction, Different Behavior

This lesson is a repeat of lesson 1. The only difference is that you'll be working on a different behavior.

Procedure:

1. Bring your dog into the training area.

2. Place the distraction out of your dog's reach.

3. Have two cookies in your hand.

4. Request a different behavior. If you have been working on sit, then maybe you'd like to do a down, or a few seconds of loose leash walking, or maybe a recall. As a side note, if you choose a recall, make a point of standing so that your dog is traveling away from the distraction rather than heading towards it. This is the only way that we can be sure that your dog is actually coming to you as opposed to heading to the counter.

5. Reward success with two cookies as described above.

6. Admire the distraction if your dog fails, then try again.

Brito works on his recall AWAY from the distraction.

Lesson #3: New Distractions

This lesson introduces new distractions! Use low-level distractions at first, then slowly raise the value. Don't forget to raise the value of your motivator, too!

Procedure:
1. Bring your dog into the training area.
2. Place the distraction out of your dog's reach.
3. Have two cookies in your hand.
4. Request an easy behavior.
5. Reward success with two cookies.
6. Admire the distraction if your dog fails, then try again.
7. Repeat this lesson, varying the distraction.

You'll need a variety of distractions.

Lesson #4: Moving Dog, Stationary Distraction

We're going to make the task a bit harder now, so the first time you do this lesson, go back to your low-level distraction. You can increase the value of the distraction once your dog has gotten the hang of it.

Procedure:
1. Put the distraction in its usual spot while your dog is watching.
2. Move the dog to a new location in the training area.
3. Request a behavior.
4. If she's successful, reward using two treats and then move to another location in the training area and repeat.
5. If she's not successful, go look at the distraction together. Then, choose a spot that is halfway between your usual training spot that you used in previous lessons, and the spot you just used. Remember, make the task easier if your dog fails!
6. Repeat 5-10 times, each time moving to a new location in the training area.

Place the distraction in the usual space.

Move to a new location and ask for a behavior.

Reward the behavior.

Give the second treat farther from the distraction.

Move to a new location and repeat.

Lesson #5: Stationary Dog, Moving Distraction

Don't forget that when you start a new lesson and make the task harder, you should make the distraction a bit easier to ignore. You can increase the value of the distraction once your dog has gotten the hang of it.

Procedure:

1. This time, instead of you and your dog moving around the training area, return to your original location.

2. Place the distraction in a different (but still inaccessible) location.

3. If your dog succeeds, great! Reward with the two-treat method, then move the distraction and do it again.

4. If your dog fails, that's okay. In fact, it's likely. Dogs do not generalize well, and this is a pretty big change. Do not tell your dog no, simply admire the distraction and then try again.

Brito practices his down cue.

Lesson #6: A Little Bit Closer

This lesson will be moving the distraction closer to the dog, which requires a way to control the distraction so your dog can't get to it! One way would be to place it in a sealed container. This is where you'll need to know your dog. If you have a five pound dog, then you can probably just place the distraction in a plastic baggie - if your dog grabs it, you'll be able to get it back very easily because very small dogs just aren't that fast at opening things with their mouths. But if you have an 80 pound lab, then don't try the baggie - she will eat the whole thing, food and baggie, in one fell swoop, without stopping to ask if it was even tasty. Another option is a nylon stocking pulled over the container. For a stronger dog, or one who is very determined, try something sturdier like a large plastic food storage container.

Note: If you read the above paragraph and felt a little queasy because you do not think that you can safely take something away from your dog, please stop reading this book and get help. If you have any concerns about being bitten, then training your dog to ignore distractions should be the least of your worries. You have a dog with another issue that needs to be worked through first. Thankfully, this issue - called resource guarding - can be solved, but you're going to need to consult a professional dog trainer who can help you.

A nylon stocking can be pulled over the distraction dish.

Procedure:

1. While your dog is watching, place your controlled distraction somewhere closer to her. For example, set it on a chair or a low shelf so it is closer to your dog's eye level.

2. Ask your dog for a simple behavior.

3. If she is successful, reward her using the two-treat method.

4. If she isn't, admire the distraction together, then try again.

5. Repeat 5-10 times per lesson, moving the distraction for each repetition.

6. In subsequent lessons, you can slowly increase the value of the distraction, change the way you stand in relation to the distraction, and work with different behaviors.

Practice simple behaviors next to the contained treat!

Lesson #7: Endurance

This lesson introduces the concept of endurance. Choose a behavior that requires your dog to work for longer periods of time. Instead of a sit or a down, which can be completed relatively quickly, try doing a stay or some loose leash walking. Throughout this lesson, you can (and should!) choose to reward your dog during the behavior, in addtion to rewarding at the end.

Do not train for longer than 5 minutes at a time. Some dogs may breeze through this lesson in one training session, while other dogs may need to spend one or more sessions on each step. Either way is fine!

Procedure:
1. Bring your dog into your training area, place the distraction out of reach, and practice the endurance behavior.
2. Increase the value of the distraction (and your reinforcer!) and continue practicing the behavior.
3. If you've been practicing a stationary behavior, move to another area in the room.
4. Now move the distraction to different areas in the room.
5. Move the distraction closer to the dog, like you did in lesson 6.
6. Repeat each step with at least two different behaviors.

Brito practices endurance with a down stay.

Lesson #8: Uncontrolled Distraction, Controlled Dog

Your dog will need to be on leash for this lesson. Because your distraction won't be contained, make sure that when you set up for each step, the distraction is at least one foot farther away than the length of your leash.

For this lesson, ANY tightening of the leash should be considered a failure. Handle failure in the usual way: go to the distraction with your dog, admire it (but do so in a way that your dog CANNOT get it), move away, and go back to work.

Procedure:
1. Place your dog on leash and take the distraction out of the container.

2. Set the distraction out of reach and request a behavior. Reward your dog using the two-treat method if she's successful.

3. Increase the value of your distraction, keeping it out of reach, and request a behavior.

4. Move around the training area, requesting a behavior in a new location each time.

5. Stay in the same place in the training area, but move the distraction around the area.

6. Move the distraction closer to your dog.

Brito is on leash as he walks past the cookies.

Lesson #9: Uncontrolled Distraction, Uncontrolled Dog

This lesson will have both your dog and the distraction off leash, so you'll need a helper! If your dog goes for the distraction, your helper's job is to get to it first and pick it up. Your helper will then hand it to you, you will admire it, and you'll start again.

Procedure:
1. Bring your dog into the area off leash. Put the uncontrolled distraction at a distance from your dog. Request a behavior and reward success with the two-treat method.

2. Increase the value of the distraction and request a behavior.

3. Move around the training area, requesting a behavior in a new location each time.

4. Stay in the same place in the training area, but move the distraction around the area.

5. Move the distraction closer to your dog and request a behavior.

6. Repeat all steps with a variety of helpers.

Brito holds his stay while looking at the cookies! Note that the helper is ready to assist if needed.

Brito does his recall past the cookies on the floor!

Lesson #10: Putting it All Together

Up until now, you've only asked for one behavior per training session. That changes now! You will be requesting several different behaviors in the same session in this lesson.

Procedure:

1. Start with your distraction controlled. Set the distraction out of reach, request a behavior, and reward with the two-treat method. Repeat, but this time ask for a different behavior. Use both quick behaviors like sit and endurance behaviors like stay. Remember to reward using the two-treat method after each behavior!

2. Increase the value of the distraction, and ask for several different behaviors.

3. Move around the training area. In each new location, ask for several different behaviors.

4. Stay in the same place in the training area, but move the distraction around. Remember to ask for a different behavior on each rep.

5. Move the distraction closer to your dog. Work several different behaviors.

6. Put your dog on leash, remove your distraction from its container, and repeat steps 1 through 5.

7. Take the leash off, use an uncontrolled distraction, and repeat steps 1 through 5. You'll need a helper for this step!

Congratulations! You've worked through all ten lessons! Your dog has been able to ignore a variety of distractions, both controlled and uncontrolled, and while both on leash and off!

Chapter 8
Changing Locations

You did a lot of great work in the last two chapters, and now your dog knows that he can follow your cues even when there are distractions present! But… well, he can only do it when he's in the same old place. That would be fine if he never left your training room, but real life doesn't work like that. This chapter will help him learn that he can perform in any location.

Benny is able to sit for a cookie on the trail.
He is ready for distraction training here.

First, take this test with your dog:

In a NEW training location, with your reward in your hand and no distractions present, ask your dog to perform a behavior for you.

If your dog does this quickly and with no more than two requests, all is well! You can proceed with this chapter.

But if your dog simply looks at you with a gently wagging tail as if he has absolutely no idea what you might be talking about, then he's not ready for you to introduce more distractions. Instead, practice your basic behaviors in a variety of locations without distractions until you can take him to a new place, show him your delicious rewards, and request - and receive! - the desired behavior.

When you select a new training space, remember that the change should be gradual. If your regular training has always taken place in your kitchen, try moving to the living room. Work through the entire lesson plan in that room, then change locations again. How about the bedroom? The bathroom?

Once you've exhausted the options in your house, take a look at the next most gradual change that you can make. How about your porch? Backyard? Front yard? In front of your neighbor's house?

Brito works in a variety of locations.
Soon, he can perform different behaviors even with cookies and toys on the ground!

In each new training space, first test that your dog can perform with a cookie in your hand. This is important because the total number of additional distractions (beyond what you are deliberately introducing) is going to increase simply by changing locations. You will continue to create controlled distractions for your dog, and you want them to hold his attention more than the stuff in the environment. This might sound counterintuitive, but the truth is, if the dog is paying more attention to the smells in the neighborhood than to the training exercises, you have a problem! You need to start with a distraction (and a reward) that is MORE interesting than the rest of the world.

If you introduce new places thoughtfully, they should be dull enough that your dog can work off leash or with a loose leash with his total attention on either you or on the distraction that you have provided. Realistically, though, sometimes you'll overestimate the draw of a new place. Therefore, your location needs to be safe as well. Your dog needs to be contained in some way, which means that for some locations, you may need to use a leash during all ten steps. You don't want to put your dog in danger in the name of training! It is much better to work on leash with a focused dog than to work off leash with a dog who is not the least bit interested in doing anything with you.

Magic and Trinity are practicing in public. They wear leashes for safety!

You should also think about the type of places you eventually want to take your dog. If your goal is to bring your dog to the pet store, to pick your children up from school, to attend local soccer games with your kids, and to walk through your neighborhood on a loose leash, then those are the places you should be using for training! Consider each of these possible locations and rank them from least distracting to most. Start with the easiest ones and work your way up.

Practice in all of the places that you will take your dog!

There's a huge advantage to using places for training that you already go to: it's efficient! You're already going there, so you won't need to spend a lot of time making special trips for the dog's training. When you head to the local school to pick up your kids, arrive ten minutes early so you can practice your skills while it's still relatively quiet. Work your way up to practicing when the kids are being released from their classrooms! Or, if you need to purchase groceries, bring your dog along for a few minutes of training outside the doors. It is much easier to stick to a training plan if it doesn't take a lot of extra time.

At first it will feel very strange to be carrying a baggie with distraction treats while you work with your dog in public, but you'll soon find that people will enjoy watching you, and might even want to know more about what you are doing!

Make a point of using friends and strangers for your distraction babysitters - we want your dog to believe that all people are willing to help you! Handle failure quietly and cheerfully; simply show your dog the delicious morsels that he won't be getting, put them back, and try again.

Most dogs will make tremendous progress working this way. After ten minutes a day for a few weeks, you will likely find that your dog is ignoring a variety of distractions that you provide in all sorts of locations. If you add this to the three or so hours you've already spent, you'll have invested around six hours, and with excellent results!

Uh oh. Too much distraction! The leash keeps Fievel safe while his trainer finds the best places to practice.

Don't despair if your dog needs a slower route. Remember that training is a process where you are developing a deeper bond with your dog. Stay focused on the journey!

Fievel is working at the perfect level of distraction for a successful sit stay.

Now get to work. You'll be completing the entire plan presented in the previous chapter, but now you will work in new places. Start small - in your house! Then your own yard. Then the school and the grocery store.... Remember, change only one thing at a time. Provide the distractions at first, and as your dog shows an ability to function then we can allow the world to provide unexpected distractions. At that point, make sure that whatever reward you have to offer is better than whatever the world might have to offer. Remember, we want our dogs to succeed!

Chapter 9
Getting Cookies Off Your Body

Do you want to hold a cookie in your hand forever?

Now that your dog is showing a lot of progress both at home and out in public, even with distractions in the environment, let's talk about that cookie that you're clutching in your hand.

In the last two chapters, you were instructed to keep two reward cookies in your hand. That was intentional so it would be obvious to your dog why it was in her best interest to cooperate! And anyway, it's likely that you created some of those behaviors with a cookie in your hand, so we wanted to keep the training picture as familiar as possible.

But now we need to change that practice of having highly visible cookies in your hand. If you're not convinced that we need to do that, ask yourself these questions:

1. Do you really want to carry a cookie in your hand forever?

2. What's your plan if you don't happen to have a cookie?

3. What if your dog does the math and decides that what the world has to offer is better than what you are holding?

Riley and Stella do not require a visible cookie to understand that one might be available!

Good training REQUIRES that we get that cookie out of your hand, even if you find yourself clinging to it like a life preserver. We want to turn your dog into an optimistic gambler, and that's not possible when you're waving a paycheck right in front of your dog's nose.

Getting the cookies off your body will require you to repeat the lesson plan several times. Don't worry - for most dogs, this will be quick because by this time your dog will be generalizing the habit of cooperation (we'll talk more about that in Part 3).

Round 1: Pocket Those Cookies!
For this set of lessons, head back to your familiar training location. We always make things easier when we change a variable in the training, and this time, that variable is the cookies in your hand.

Start with your regular setup at Lesson 1, only this time, instead of keeping the cookies in your hand as you train, show them to your dog, then place those cookies in your pocket. Request a behavior.

Success? Take the cookies out of your pocket and give them to your dog as usual.

Failure? Pull the cookies out of your pocket and show them to your dog. This should feel familiar because in the past you did exactly the same thing with the distraction. Now we're going to show the dog both the distraction (lower value) and the cookie that she just missed out on (higher value). Of course, we are simply showing - not giving. "This is the cookie you won't be getting."

Loba is practicing without a cookie in Erika's hand.

Loba failed to "sit" on cue so Erika shows her the cookie from her pocket. The cookie still exists!

Round 2: Cookies Across the Room

You're going to repeat all of the lessons again, but this time, show your dog the cookie and then place it somewhere else in the room instead of your pocket. The cookies should be placed on the opposite side of the room from the distraction. This way, you will be moving away from the distraction when your dog earns the reward.

Loba is now working for a cookie across the room.

Loba did it! Erika gives her the bowl with a few treats as her reward.

Now, request a behavior. If your dog fails, go and show your dog what she missed out on and start over. If your dog succeeds, go with your dog to the location of the reinforcer, and give her some! She worked hard; she earned it!

Most dogs will work through both of these steps (cookie in pocket and cookie across the room) in just a few days. Now it's time to truly introduce the idea of gambling.

Round 3: No Visible Rewards!

Next time you train, place the cookies somewhere in the room BEFORE you get your dog. Do not show your dog the cookie before you begin the training session. This time, when you ask for a behavior, your dog is truly gambling. She doesn't know what - if anything! - you have to offer.

Success? Go and get the cookie and give it to your dog. Heck, give her several - that was hard work! Don't forget to add in some heartfelt and enthusiastic praise as you give her each of those cookies!

Loba sits on cue and....   *Her reward comes from the refrigerator!*

Failure? Go and get the cookies and show them to your dog. But instead of simply repeating the lesson, take the dog out of the room and start over. This is important or you'll set yourself up for a lifetime of "show me the money" before your dog will do any work.

In fact, you will remove your dog from the room after each repetition - whether it was a success or a failure - so you can move the location of the reward cookies. Bring your dog in the room and start another repetition. If your dog decides to ignore you and walk around the room looking for your stash, no problem. Show her the cookies that you are not going to give her, take her out of the room, and start over again.

Some dogs will get stuck at this stage for a few days. No worries - they'll get it! Other dogs will not make a mistake from step one. Wonderful!

Round 4: No Visible Cookies in the Real World

Now take that training out into the world! You will need to do a bit of planning in advance at this stage. In addition to placing your distraction in the new training area, you'll also be placing your reward somewhere in that area as well. To save time, you can place treats in four or five locations before you bring the dog into the area. That way you can simply move from stash to stash in order to reward.

Round 5: Gambling for Quality of Reinforcers

This step requires that you take a test first: Take your dog to a new location away from home. Place an attractive distraction on the ground, either loosely contained or with a babysitter. Bring your dog into the area with no treats on your body - they should already be hidden in the area. Cue a behavior. If your dog can succeed without tightening the leash, it's time to introduce the idea of gambling for the quality of reinforcers.

Which reward will Loba gets if she succeeds?
Teach your dog to "gamble" for their favorites!

For the first time, the value of the treats that you use as motivators are not going to remain constant. Instead, I want you to get a bowl of motivators with different values. If you are planning on doing ten repetitions, then you should have twenty treats available that range in value from 1 to 10 - two of each value.

Place a distraction with a value of about 5 in your training area. Bring your dog into the training area and proceed as normal, but this time your dog will get whatever comes out of the bowl, which may or may not be a higher value option than the distraction that your dog is ignoring. When you place your hand in the treat bowl, neither one of you should know what might come out.

Gambling like this is highly effective with ALL learners! And while it may seem counterintuitive, the reality is that dogs will work harder and harder when they are gambling. Just like humans, they like that tiny bit of uncertainty; it drives determination and hope. Will this attempt bring a small reward, or is this going to be the big jackpot? We'll take advantage of this as we move forward through the rest of this book.

Before we continue, though, let's consider how much total training time you've actually spent. If you are working with your dog twice a day for about five minutes each time, most dogs will be entering their third month of training. That means a total of about nine hours of training time. Not a bad return on investment!

Chapter 10
Reducing Cookies with Life Rewards

*Ursa offers a quiet sit. She knows that this is required to
be released for a swim.*

We need to start thinking about how to reduce the number of cookies
we use in training. We will start doing this by considering non-food
rewards. The reason is simple: we want to deeply incorporate our
formal training into real life. Not only does this allow us to get away
from needing pockets full of cookies, but it also allows us a way to train
(and win) when the value of whatever is in the environment is greater
than what we have to offer. Then, in the next chapter, we'll work on
requiring the dog to complete multiple behaviors for one cookie.
But first, let's look at the three main types of rewards that we can offer
our dogs.

First up, food. Food is an obvious choice of motivator for most dogs.
Until now, we have focused exclusively on using food in our training
because it is highly effective, convenient, and easy to use correctly.
Most dogs are naturally interested in food. Food is a great option
when a dog is just learning a behavior, especially when the behavior
is being taught via clicker training or shaping activities, because it is
easy to offer a large quantity of rewards in a very short period of time.
Unfortunately, this ease of use means that you can become overly
reliant on food if you do not develop a plan to reduce its use.

This group of dogs sits quietly. They are hoping for a cookie!

Next on the list is toys. Some dogs love their toys and will work very hard for a chance to play, while other dogs have no interest in toys at all. But even for dogs who play well, toys are a challenge to use in training because each repetition takes a good deal of time to complete. While a cookie can be eaten in seconds, even a quick game with a toy will take

This dog sits quietly until released. His reward is a game of fetch in the lake!

at least fifteen seconds each time you want to reward your dog.

Finally, we have life rewards. These are things that your dog wants or needs on a daily basis, simply as part of being alive. We can teach a dog that getting what he wants is contingent on us getting what we want. Want to go outside? Sit politely first. Want to enter the dog park? Walk quietly on a loose leash to the entrance. Want to chase that squirrel? Hold your sit stay until you are released. If you think about it, you'll realize that there are many training opportunities built into each day if you take advantage of life rewards.

Cloud controls his impulse to run out the door to the car. Cloud understands the value of cooperation.

Life rewards teach two basic principles to your dog. First, that he can control his impulses, and indeed, that he must do so in order to get what he wants. Second, life rewards help your dog understand that doing things for you is the key to getting his needs and wants met. If your dog wishes to do something enjoyable, like go outside or go for a car ride, then he must offer a desired behavior first. This creates a habit of checking in with you when he wants something.

Life rewards are especially potent with independent dogs. If you control the things that your independent dog wants, then you matter more to him, and you have a very good chance of controlling his behavior.

Life rewards can be difficult to put into practice at times; you're not going to wait for your puppy to sit before you open the back door if you're trying to potty train him! So pick and choose which ones make sense for your situation.

The first step to using life rewards in training is allowing your dog to have the distraction. Yes, you read that right. That thing that your dog has wanted all along? We're going to let him have it.

...but there's a catch: he has to do something for you first.
To introduce this concept, start by setting up your normal training

Stella wants to run in the snow. First she is asked to recall directly to her trainer, and her reward is a chance to run free!

area with a controlled distraction and an additional pile of equal-value rewards somewhere else in the room. Bring your dog into the room and request a behavior. by this time, your dog must be an obedience expert, so he should nail your request almost instantly. Instead of going to your stash of motivators, though, walk right over to the distraction and give part of it your dog. This will communicate to your dog, "If you do something for me, sometimes I will give you the exact thing that you wanted."

 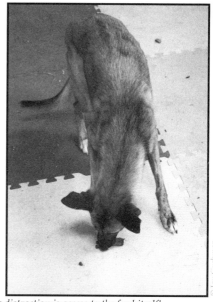

Joy's reward for working in the presence of a distraction is access to the food itself!

After you complete that first repetition, work through the lesson plan once more, this time giving your dog rewards from either your hidden stash of treats, or by giving him access to the distraction itself. The trick here is to be absolutely certain that your dog is not helping himself to the distraction; you are the one giving him access to it! Make your release very clear: sweep your hand forward, let your dog go ahead of you, and open up the container so that he can access the distraction.

Work through this process in a variety of locations until your dog clearly understands the basic rule: cooperate with your owner and get what you want… maybe even the distraction itself!

Now we're going to raise criteria again. This time, instead of setting up a training scenario, allow life to offer you one naturally. If your dog wants to go outside, ask him to sit first. If he doesn't, simply walk away for a minute. Then try again. On your first efforts, you might find yourself asking 10 or more times before your dog complies - but he will do it! Don't push your luck, though. Once you get the behavior, open the door! A quick reward will make your point much faster than asking for a two minute stay.

The next time you ask your dog to sit before going out the door, see what happens. I bet his butt pops straight to the ground. Great, now add a new behavior before opening the door. Still good? Ask for a small amount of endurance - can he stay for three seconds? Super! Go ahead and open the door!

Now, another change. This time, ask for the behavior and then start to open the door. If your dog breaks before you clearly released him, shut the door. That's right: change your mind. Make it clear to your dog that throwing himself through the small opening is not going to work. Most dogs can learn to wait patiently in just a day or two- even with the door open wide in front of them.

Finally, generalize this concept. For example, when your dog wants to go for a walk, ask for a polite sit before you reach down to attach the leash. If he pops up, stop what you are doing. Start over. The first day you might spend more time trying to get the leash on than you do walking, but on the second day, you'll think you have a new dog! Now he will be sitting politely when you attach the leash. He might be vibrating, but he'll be vibrating politely!

If you perform distraction training wisely, you'll be able to call your dog off a tree with a squirrel in it.
Just remember - let the dog go back to the distraction if it's safe!

Where else can you use this concept? It will depend on your dog. Ask yourself what your dog wants in life. Your dog wants to swim? He has to perform for you first. No work means no swim. Your dog wants dinner? Well, you want him to sit and stay while you place it on the ground. He breaks his stay? No bowl of food. Your dog wants to chase that squirrel? Expect him to walk on a loose leash past the tree before you'll let him go - but don't push your luck with behaviors that require a good deal of endurance and self control, such as waiting to chase a squirrel. Dogs get it, and they usually get it very, very quickly.

Before we move on, let's take a quick look back. If you've completed all of the steps presented so far in this book, you should have a dog who will work under distraction, in a variety of locations, and both with and without motivators on your body. You have a dog who will offer polite behaviors even when you don't have any food available at all, simply for a chance to engage in activities that he enjoys on a daily basis. And odds are excellent that you have invested less than twelve hours of training time! What a deal!

Chapter 11
Reducing Cookies: Show Me More

If you've worked through the preceding chapters, you have an amazing dog who can perform in a wide variety of circumstances… if you give her a cookie every single time. Now it's time for one more form of gambling for your dog: not knowing how many behaviors she might have to complete before earning a reinforcer.

Dogs that perform in competitions do many behaviors under distraction.

To do this, we will introduce behavior chains to your dog. A behavior chain is a series of behaviors performed one after the other for a reward. A simple example of a behavior chain would be a sit, stay (while you cross the room), and a recall - all performed in a row for just one cookie. Instead of giving the dog a reward for each behavior (sit, stay, and come), we want more bang for our buck, so to speak. We want to use just one cookie for all three of those behaviors.

Go back to your familiar training area with no distractions (or food) visible. Ask your dog for a single behavior. This should be easy based on all of the work you've already done. When you get the behavior, tell your dog she's wonderful! Then, instead of giving her a cookie, quickly ask for another behavior. Once that behavior has been completed, reward her! That cookie just got you two behaviors for the price of one.

It's time to go back to the lesson plan, but this time you won't ask for a single behavior. Instead, you'll ask for anywhere between one and ten behaviors before offering a reward. Your dog must not know just how many behaviors you have in mind; we're creating the ultimate gambler. Indeed, you can have your dog working very hard and with a wonderful attitude, under distraction, for minutes at a time - if you increase the level of challenge slowly and systematically.

And if your dog fails? Start over from the beginning. If you were striving for five behaviors and failure took place after three, you still want to ask for five on the next repetition. In this case, if you make the work easier, your dog will not learn to keeping trying and stay in the game under growing adversity.

Does this really work - even in real life?

Bazil loves her training! She doesn't mind the wait between cookies.

To answer this question, let's go back to those dogs you see on TV. I'm talking about the extremely well-trained dogs who perform a variety of routines in public, under pressure, and without reinforcers. The truth is, those dogs always get treats. Forever. No effort is ever made to wean them off the treats, because their trainers place tremendous value on having dogs who will perform with great enthusiasm and speed no matter what. But the dog will NEVER earn cookies in the competition ring. Ever.

This is possible because the trainers turn their dogs into extremely optimistic gamblers. In training, the dog might get rewarded for performing one behavior, but she might also have to work for several minutes before being rewarded. The reward might be a cookie, a toy, or incredibly enthusiastic praise, but something will happen to let that dog know that she was brilliant and that her trainer is very proud! Sometimes the rewards come at the beginning of a session and sometimes at the end. Most of the time they are totally random, sprinkled throughout the session. And sometimes there will be no rewards at all in a specific session, because that's part of being random. But the next session might be full of rewards! The dog knows that, and so she keeps working hard.

If you want fast, crisp, enthusiastic work under distraction, you have exactly one choice: continue to reward what you like on a variable reinforcement schedule so that your dog doesn't know how long she will have to work to get her motivator. That's it.

For your purposes, this means that your dog might have to perform ten behaviors to get a cookie, or maybe you'll only ask for one. If you're wondering how that translates to the real world, you need to know that those rewardable behaviors do not have to be sequential. They do not have to occur one after the other, or even on the same day.

If you call your dog to come in the house from the yard three days in a row, you can pick which of those times you want to reward. Maybe one of them, or maybe all three. But your dog will have no way of knowing which time she will be rewarded because the cookie is not even on your body anymore. You have access to that cookie, and that is the only thing that your dog needs to know. If you want to come up with a cookie, you will. If you don't want to come up with a cookie, you won't.

If your dog has no way of knowing what you are (or are not) offering for any given request, then she will keep trying because this time might be the winner! Better yet, because you taught her to be a gambler when it comes to the quality of the reinforcer as well, if you pull an old, dehydrated cookie from three days ago out of your pocket, your dog will accept that. And if you have a leftover chicken breast from last night's dinner as an extra special surprise, well, she'll be thrilled about that for sure! She just hit the jackpot!

Be careful with those super special treats. If jackpots become common, they lose their surprising effect, so they need to stay rare and exciting. This is similar to how you would feel if you won the jackpot at a casino! Too many jackpots and they would begin to feel ho hum. Worse yet, the next time you won only a couple bucks, you'd be disappointed.

These dogs are optimistic gamblers. They hold their stay even though they are not sure if they will earn a reward.

What about physical corrections? If we hit both ends of the spectrum by rewarding our dogs when they do what we want and also punishing what we don't want, does that help?

Train your dog to perform willingly, even when off leash and out of your reach.

While it might seem logical, the answer is no. Corrections only work if you can reach your dog. If you use a leash correction, then you need your dog to be on leash. If you do not have a leash on the dog, you'll need to go get her or call her to you in order to punish her. In this case, it's likely that your dog will begin to avoid you. And if that happens, you really do have a problem because dogs are generally faster than humans. Trying to catch a dog during a game of keepaway is the definition of frustration.

What about an electronic collar? Same problem. It only works if your dog is wearing it. Not much fun to keep a special collar on your pet dog 24 hours a day for the rest of her life. But access to those cookies in your fridge? Yep, you have access to them 24 hours a day, 7 days a week. Plus, you can go get them AFTER the behavior, so you can make your decision about whether or not to reward your dog after the fact.

What a deal!

If you want tons of reliability, in a variety of environments, and under challenging conditions, then you'll have to train your dog - and you'll have to make it worth her while to cooperate with you. Give your dog a reason to cooperate, and then put that reason (the reinforcer) on a highly random reward schedule so that your dog is endlessly gambling.

Chapter 12
When the Distractions Aren't Food

Sometimes the distraction is not food. Here Tru and Blayze want to swim, but they have learned to wait politely for permission.

As you read through the prior chapters, you probably noticed that the training plan is laid out to be slow, systematic, and thorough. Your dog has been taught to perform in the presence of obvious distractions that you provided. He's been asked to perform in new locations. And he's learned to be an optimistic gambler who works for both the occasional, unpredictable cookie and for general life rewards. Wow!

But if you have sensed that there's a piece missing, you're right!

The truth is, the world is not a controlled place, and not all distractions are about food. Sometimes your dog will want a ball that someone is bouncing in the distance. Sometimes your dog will want to greet a nearby friend. Sometimes your dog will simply be overwhelmed by the sheer number of options available! So how do we prepare our dogs for this eventuality?

Exactly the same way.

In much the same way that we develop a sense of what attracts our human children over time, you will develop a sense of what attracts your dog as well.

Does your dog love to greet new people? Wonderful! As you approach a new person and your dog starts to pull, stop moving. Allow your dog to notice the change. When your dog looks back at you, ask for a simple behavior like sit. Then proceed towards the distracting person with a loose leash. If your dog pulls, start over again! Take your time. When you reach the person, your dog's reward for loose leash walking is a chance to greet the other person - a life reward that is highly desirable to your dog! If your dog is an overly enthusiastic greeter, help your dog be successful by feeding cookies dropped on the ground to make it less likely that your dog will jump up.

Obviously if your dog fails and tightens the leash, you will not show the person to your dog to remind him of what he is working for (the way you did with the cookies), but he will figure that out very easily. Simply continuing to move towards that person will be the reminder of success, and not moving forward, or even backing up, will signal the need to try again.

As we did before, set up situations for your dog to learn this! Ask your friends, family, neighbors, and anyone who wants to greet your dog if they would help you by waiting patiently as you move towards them on a loose leash. Most people are very happy to help if you just tell them what you need from them.

Jib practices waiting politely at the front door with no distractions.
Start small and build up!

How about at the front door? Your doorbell has rung and your dog is struggling to hold his stay. Set that up too! Have your friends and family ring the doorbell. Ask your dog to sit and stay. When you open the door, allow your dog to make a choice. If your dog hops up, shut the door and start over. Soon, your dog will wait while you open the door.

But is that a good place to start for his first lesson on sitting nicely at the front door? NO! Break it down into little pieces and work your way up. How about putting your dog on leash and ringing the doorbell yourself while you reward your dog for a quiet sit? Then add opening and closing the door to your plan. Then add a bit of endurance to that stay. And finally, add new people to the picture.

Maybe people are not what cause your dog to get excited; maybe it's toys or balls instead! When your dog watches children playing ball, does he want to take their ball? You can set this up yourself.

Tru and Blayze practice waiting politely at the gate. They will be rewarded for their good manners with a chance to grab their toys!

Start by completing the entire training plan again, this time using a beloved toy instead of food. Start small! Your first lessons will be in a quiet location, not at the ball game. Practicing in your backyard is a great idea. That way, when your dog is correct, you can throw a second ball that you are holding on your body. Proceed from there - ball visible in your hand, ball in your pocket, ball placed on a table nearby, and so on.

When your dog is a star with a non-moving ball on the ground, add movement! Ask a helper to start by gently moving the ball while you reward your dog's good decisions with big throws of a ball. Work your way to the point where your dog can focus on you even when other people are playing ball nearby - always rewarding the dog generously for his efforts.

Now you can take these games on the road! When you attend your child's baseball game, make sure that you bring a ball along. Start far away from the actual game to help your dog succeed. Let your dog work on a long line of 30 feet or more to guarantee that your dog won't run off and join the baseball game at an inopportune moment. Over time, your dog will learn to watch games nearby without reacting. Indeed, your dog will look to you for a chance to see what you have instead.

Great sit! Here comes your ball!

When that happens, it's time to randomize those rewards. Sometimes your dog's calm behavior in the presence of distractions will earn a cookie. Sometimes your dog's good behavior will earn praise. Sometimes you'll take your dog a safe distance away and play ball yourself! And if you're very lucky, maybe the reward will be a life reward - your dog will be allowed to join the game and catch a ball or two!

Most dogs have a few notable "distraction triggers." The above examples are maybe the most common, but think about what is most distracting to YOUR dog. Now create a plan for those triggers. Consider intensity, proximity, and distance in your plan. If you've already worked through the plan in Chapter 7 using food, this will likely go very quickly. Remember to change as few variables at a time as possible.

Dogs can learn to cooperate even under very trying conditions, but it takes some effort and thought to create a plan that makes sense for your situation. Training your dog is a journey that allows both of you to live in harmony. Enjoy the process of helping your dog learn to live successfully in the world with you! Rather than thinking of training as something you just need to get done, think of training as a lifelong journey where you both begin to relate to each other on a deeper and richer level.

Working slowly and consistently, your dog can learn to cooperate under very challenging conditions.

Chapter 13
Off-leash Reliability

So far, I haven't said too much about using a leash or not using one. If you think about it, the leash is mostly irrelevant to the entire plan that I have laid out for you. It should not have mattered if your dog was on leash or not (except when you were working with uncontrolled distractions and you needed the leash to prevent your dog from getting to them).

But in the real world, we want our dogs to have the ability to be off leash when it's safe and legal, which means they need to be reliable around uncontrolled distractions. This chapter will help you make that transition.

Let's take a quick inventory so that we that we know where we're at:

- So far, you've been using a helper when your dog is off leash around an uncontrolled distraction. Does your helper no longer have a job?

- Is your dog so reliable that the helper no longer needs to step in to prevent your dog from getting the distraction?

- When you don't have a helper available, you've been keeping your dog on leash around uncontrolled distractions. Are you at the point where your leash no longer tightens - not even once - before your dog remembers you? Does your dog look at a distraction and immediately turn back to see what she needs to do to get it?

- We've talked about the idea of variable reinforcement. Is your dog willing to gamble? Does she accept that reinforcement may not happen for every behavior, and as a result, works even harder on the next attempt?

- Finally, you've been using life rewards. Does your dog understand that cooperation with you is the only way to get access to everyday needs and wants? Is your dog willing to sit politely and wait for a release when she wants to go outside?

Is your dog maintaining a loose leash during training?

If you answered yes to all of these questions, you're probably ready to work off leash. But before you do, ask yourself one more time: are you truly ready to remove the leash? If your dog is consistently keeping the leash loose regardless of what is happening around you, then you're ready, and in your heart you probably already knew that.

However, if you're like most people, you probably have some doubts or are worried about what might happen. Leave the leash on. It's better to keep your safety net in place even if you don't need it than to hope for the best, remove the leash, and have your dog develop bad habits. So now, let's talk about how to bridge the gap from leash to no leash.

Start by training in a safe, boring, and contained area with no obvious distractions. An enclosed tennis court or a friend's fenced yard are good

If you're transitioning to off leash work, consider letting the leash hang without holding the end as a first step.

examples of a suitable space. Before you ask for any work, allow your dog plenty of time to explore the new space - at least fifteen minutes. By allowing her to satisfy her curiosity, your first foray into off leash work is likely to be highly successful!

Acre is practicing advanced obedience skills in a safely contained area.

Now go back to the lesson plan. Your lessons should go extremely quickly since your dog has followed this path many times before. Work on all your behaviors, but focus your energy on reliable stays and recalls since these are the two skills that will be most valuable when your dog is off leash.

When working recalls, make a point of using a really good reinforcer, one that your dog thinks is amazing, and possibly something so special that it is only used for recalls. Introduce distractions by placing them outside the fence (preventing your dog from helping herself), and the first few times your dog successfully leaves those distractions to come to you, offer a jackpot. We want your dog to be extremely positive about her new freedom!

Luna is wearing her leash. That will make it much easier to catch her if she breaks her stay command!

When it's time to end the session, call your dog to you, give her a delicious morsel, and attach the leash. But instead of leaving immediately, drop the leash so that your dog is dragging it behind her while she does a few more minutes of exploration or work. This is very important! If your dog learns that recalls are associated with a leash and a loss of freedom, then you will likely kill your recall very quickly. When it's time to go, don't call her. Instead, go to your dog, hand her another cookie, pick up the leash, and leave.

In your next training session, head back to a contained area, but this time you're going to take a few risks. After she's had a chance to investigate, call her to you and let her watch as you place a distraction on the ground. The distraction is freely available - your dog is off leash, after all, and she might choose to ignore you - so make a point to use a low-value distraction and have very high-value rewards. With the distraction in full view and with your dog off leash, return to your dog and proceed with your lessons as usual.

What happened?

First this Australian Shepherd practices off leash in a contained space.

Next he practices off leash in public. And he does great!

If your dog worked as she has been trained to do, ignoring the distraction and happily responding to your cues in hopes of either receiving a cookie from you or being allowed to access the distraction, then all is well. Your dog gets it. You'll spend a few weeks increasing the value of the distraction, working in new locations, and changing how often you reinforce, as in the gambler scenario.

And if your dog failed? That's okay. You haven't ruined her training, you've simply learned that your dog is not quite ready for that level of responsibility. Go get your dog gently, give her several cookies to prevent her from avoiding you in the future, and think back. Be honest with yourself; was your dog truly ready for this step, or did you rush various stages of training? It's okay if you moved too fast - it happens to the best of us. Just back up a bit, find the hole in your training, work through it, and then try again.

Sometimes while doing this kind of training, some uncontrolled distraction will appear, like a squirrel in a tree. What should you do? This is a very challenging situation for your dog, so ask for one repetition of your dog's easiest behavior, and then release her to chase the critter. If you give your dog permission to go away from you (to chase a squirrel), then you also have a much better chance of getting your dog back when you call. It will also appear to your dog that you controlled that situation- that squirrel was just one more distraction! You will find that your dog will turn to you more and more quickly for permission to access an uncontrolled distraction in the environment.

Extreme reliability under a range of circumstances is not a matter of a few months of training, although that is a good start. Extreme reliability is a lifestyle that includes consistent training and effort, with ever-increasing challenges to overcome.

Some people will find that they own highly cooperative dogs who quickly overcome every possible challenge in a matter of weeks, while others will find that their dogs are more intense, independent, or determined to find their own entertainment. All dogs can be trained, but some will be able to reach higher levels of reliability than others. This is well known and understood by all professional trainers.

While you need to accept your dog for the unique being that she is, if you put in the training time, the vast majority of dogs can be trained to a reasonable level of reliability. Still, if you have one of those impulsive dogs who struggles to pay attention to you, do not place your dog or others at risk when you make choices about your training situations. If you do not feel confident about your dog's off leash reliability, then keep the leash on!

You can help make the transition easier by letting your dog drag a long line that is 30 or 40 feet long until you feel absolutely confident that your dog's responsiveness is a function of your training and your relationship as opposed to the leash. Some owners prefer to take a gradual approach to removing the leash, shortening it a few feet at a time until it's just a few inches hanging from the dog's collar. That's okay too! The more comfort and confidence that you possess, the more your dog will follow your lead.

Finally, congratulations are in order. You have taken your dog from only obeying you when you had a cookie in your hand and there was nothing else going on to a dog who can be safely off leash in a variety of situations, even if you don't have an obvious reward at hand. And all told, it was probably less than 20 to 30 hours of work, spread out in 5 minute increments. That's amazing!

Now go enjoy your dog!

*Off leash control is developed over time with thoughtful
and systematic training.*

Part Three:
Problem Solving

Notes

Chapter 14
Oops! How to Handle Mistakes

As we've moved through the exercises, I have suggested that you handle failure in one basic way: show your dog what you aren't going to give him, and then try again. This approach is incredibly simple and effective. If you believe that your dog knows how to perform correctly and that he is struggling because he is torn - one part of him wants to cooperate but the other just wants that distraction! - then 90% of the time, this is exactly how you should handle errors.

Is Raika failing to respond to a command because she does not know how to perform or because she is confused? The fact that she is looking right at her handler and not at the cookies suggests confusion. Help her by making it easier!

But sometimes your dog simply has no idea what you want him to do. Think back to Chapter 2, where we evaluated what a dog does or does not know. If you ask him to sit and he just stares at you, even though there is nothing else to do, you can generally assume that your dog is truly unclear on what you want. Maybe you're sitting in a chair or holding your hands in a different position than you have in the past. If your dog knew what to do to earn that delicious cookie in your hand, then he would simply do it!

In a case like this, your response to failure should be… nothing. There is no consequence at all. Instead, go back to the teaching phase and work through that behavior again. How you will do that depends on how you trained your dog in the first place. If you shaped it with a clicker, then go back to the clicker. If you lured it with a cookie, then go back to luring, with or without a cookie in your hand. How you get the behavior doesn't matter too much; just re-teach the behavior with no negative consequences for failure.

Raika is staring at the distraction. This suggests that the failure to respond is due to distraction rather than confusion.

By showing the distraction to your dog, you can often get him working again.

Sometimes, though, the dog does not respond when you ask him to sit because he's looking at something else. That's a little different. In that case, you'll go to the distraction with the dog and admire it together. This will help "unlock" the dog from staring, and it will get him working for you again. For some other dogs, the best thing is simply to wait them out. As long as they can't get to the distraction, you can wait until they turn back to you for another attempt at the behavior. If you do either of these strategies two or three times and your dog still isn't getting it right, then instead of trying the same failing strategy time and again, make the exercise easier for the dog! Go back to Chapter 4 and review the variables of intensity, proximity, and duration; change one of them, and try again!

Success is important! Here Raika turned away from the distraction and followed the "sit" command. Time for her reward!

Being successful is important! Setting your learner up for success maintains a positive attitude, which generates more success. Allowing for repeated failure, especially if the requested behavior is not well understood, causes your learner to give up or to avoid his lessons. We want to avoid that at all costs! If he has forgotten why it is in his best interest to work hard and cooperate, reminding him of the consequences for success tends to jump start the learning process.

Here's a human example: if you were working with a child on his multiplication tables and he got one wrong, you might let him know he was wrong and then encourage him (cheerfully!) to try again. If you asked the same question five times in a row and he just guessed all over the place, you'd probably recognize that you were accomplishing absolutely nothing. Rather than continuing on a failing path, if you broke the problem down into easier parts so he could master the skill, odds are he'd be more successful.

Of course, if your student was failing because he was looking out the window where his friends were playing, wistfully wishing he could join them, odds are good that you would remind him that he could play with his friends in just a minute, after a few more correct answers. You don't have to yell, raise your voice, or get upset. You simply remind your young learner why he cares; he can take care of the rest himself by operating within his own self interest. He works harder to focus because he recognizes that doing so will get him outdoors to his friends faster, not because you forced him. By reacting in this manner, you have kept your relationship intact and you have also accomplished your goal - furthering your child's education.

Remember that learning theory applies equally across species. It doesn't matter if you're training a dog or a dolphin or a child - we all follow the laws of learning. The point is, if you see more than two failures in a row, and you believe it's because your dog doesn't understand the task, go ahead and simplify the assignment for your dog; something is wrong with the setup! If you feel that your dog's struggle is more about the distraction than a lack of understanding, then follow the first path - show the distraction, but do not give it to the dog.

Okay, so you've tried this, and it's still not working. You are sure that your dog knows what you want him to do because he responds promptly and easily to your cues when there is no challenge. You have gone to great lengths to set the dog up for success with small increments of challenge. Yet as soon as you add even a minor distraction, or when you raise the value of that distraction, you find your dog staring at it with no response to you at all. Now what?

It's time to add a reset. Failure will be followed by mutual admiration of the thing that the dog wants - and then, instead of trying again immediately, you are going to wait for up to 10 seconds before trying again. Now your dog has experienced two consequences. The first is looking at what he wants but not getting it, and the second is delay; the opportunity to try again is not going to be instant. You're going to give the dog a chance to think about it.

Still experiencing failure? End the session. This can help in several ways. If your dog is failing to perform due to stress or fear, it removes the distress. If your dog is failing to perform because the task is too difficult, then it gives you a chance to re-evaluate what is reasonable and how much you really want to ask of your dog. And finally, if your dog simply does not want to perform, then it is a way to communicate to your dog that while he does not have to cooperate, you will not be cooperating, either; the cookie will disappear. If you have selected your motivators correctly, your dog won't appreciate this response.

This will work. Your dog will begin to make different choices in the future to get that cookie! If this isn't intuitive to you, think about how you might feel if you looked at a piece of cake, but were told you couldn't have it. How would you feel if you saw the cake you were told you couldn't have, but then you were immediately given another chance to get it? How would that compare to seeing the cake, not getting it, and then having it go away altogether?

You shouldn't be using this technique very often if you are selecting appropriate environments, motivators, and levels of distraction, but no matter how hard you work to create a perfect learning environment, all dogs will make errors on occasion - and many dogs will frequently check to see if the rules still require compliance.

This method does work, but the drawback is that it is unpleasant for your dog - and we want to avoid unpleasant experiences as much as possible. Go to great lengths to set your dog up to win. It might seem like a slow way to get where you want to go, but in this case, the turtle WILL win the race. Slow and steady. Maintain a positive attitude and ensure that your dog stays willing and able to play the training game with you. If your dog becomes discouraged with the level of difficulty, then you'll set yourself back, which is no fun for either one of you.

Setting up for perfect training sessions with no errors is great in theory, but very hard to accomplish in practice. Do your best, but don't beat yourself up if you occasionally fail. You'll get better with practice.

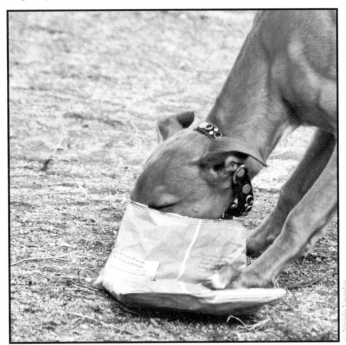

Accidents happen. It's okay.

Dealing with Human Error

Let's say you've just set up a training session and your delicious distraction is sitting on the floor near your friend. You've gone to some trouble to set the stage, explaining that you want him to cover the distraction that is on the floor if your dog goes for it. And then there is a misunderstanding. The unthinkable happens; not only does your dog fail to respond to your cue, but you also watch in horror as your helper allows your dog to eat the food and then lick each last crumb off the floor. Now what?!

Stuff happens. There's no point in worrying about a training session that's gone wrong. Yelling at your helper is futile, because then he won't work with you - and you still need that person! Yelling at your dog is futile, as well. Your dog already got the food, so at this point, yelling mostly communicates that you're a bit unpredictable and moody.

While it is true that a failure of this type gives your dog the wrong message, the important thing to consider is how many successes you've had in relation to the occasional failure. Hopefully a lot! Remaining calm and in control will do wonders for both your training and your relationship with your dog, so resist the urge to respond with anger at either the dog or the helper! Try again, possibly after a short break.

The food is gone. The past is the past. It's time to move forward.

Preventing Errors Outside of Formal Training

While you are working with your dog, you will also be living life. That means that your dog is going on walks (possibly pulling), running out the door (without holding his stays), and failing to come when you call. While you are working through your distraction training process, you will need to implement something called management.

Simply avoid the issues as much as you can. If your dog pulls on a leash and collar, purchase a front clip harness that is designed to prevent pulling. While the no-pull harness will not teach your dog to walk politely on leash, it will allow you to walk your dog without undoing

Do your best to manage your dog's behavior to prevent too many failures while you work on your distraction training.

all your good training. Your dog won't be pulling your arm off, nor will he be developing the bad habit of pulling into the collar.

If you'd like your dog to hold a stay at the door, but you need to get to work and don't have time to wait the dog out, then don't ask your dog to stay. Just open the door and let the dog go flying out. While it's not great for your overall training if you do this frequently, it's better to say nothing if you know that your dog will not respond than to give cues that are totally ignored. With time, training, and practice, all of the pieces will come together.

And when you called your dog to come in and he ignored that as well? There's not much to be done at that moment, either. Go and get your dog or go get a cookie to make it likely that he'll come back. It is true that this is generally poor training and that too much of this will wreak havoc with your long term success, but sometimes there is a place for just dealing with situations when they occur.

If you stay calm and give your dog a cookie when he shows up - even if he's completely ignored you for five minutes - your dog will still like you. If he likes you, then your training will improve his reaction time in the future. But if you scream, yell, and throw things, then your dog will become afraid of you, which will delay the point at which training and real life merge.

Next time, keep your dog on a leash until you're ready for more challenge. And while you're at it, remember to notice when your dog surprises you with an awesome, possibly unexpected response to your recall cue. If you are surprised when he comes, express that surprise by running to the fridge and finding some fabulous morsels and simultaneously making a huge fuss over him. Now you're both surprised - in a good way! And you just turned a potential management situation into a very powerful training session - one that both of you will remember and benefit from for a long time to come.

Just remember, you're the turtle. Settle in.

This dog is not ready to be off leash at this time. That's okay; keep training!

Chapter 15
When Fear Gets in the Way

This dog is trying to escape.

Fear is a prime reason why many dogs do not respond to cues, especially when they are away from home. If you've followed both the training plan in this book and my advice in the previous chapter on handling mistakes, but your dog is still struggling, fear may be to blame.

Think about what happens when you take your normally happy and engaged dog to a local training class. Does she…

- Lunge or snap at other dogs, people, or even at you?
- Try to drag you back to the car?
- Stop moving entirely, becoming frozen as if she's rooted to the spot?
- Refuse to even look at a cookie, much less eat it?
- Become entirely unrecognizable?

If so, what you are seeing is fear. Your dog is frightened by this new situation. Even friendly dogs who are used to greeting one dog or person at a time will become overwhelmed when there are twenty all crowded into a small space! Whether your dog lashes out, tries to escape, or simply goes catatonic, she is so overwhelmed by the new experience that she simply cannot function.

Fear is a response that is shared equally by humans and dogs alike, and many of the reactions are the same for both species. It's important to understand that the feeling of fear served both us humans and our dogs very well in the not-so-distant past! The ability to quickly identify and respond to threats was critical to our survival; when in doubt about how safe or dangerous a situation might be, we (rightly) erred on the side of caution.

From an evolutionary point of view, there is nothing normal about a dog sharing a small space with a large number of strange dogs and people. Your dog's fear of the unknown is very normal. It might not appear rational to you as the owner, but that's because you can understand the concept of "dog training school." From your dog's point of view, though, you have taken her into a strange situation, and she really doesn't know if she is safe or not!

Note the flattened ears and wide eyes. This dog is mildly concerned but is able to work in public.

Some dogs rarely feel fear in new circumstances. Either through excellent genetics, smart socialization, or a little of both, these dogs adapt very well to almost all new experiences. They are the first ones to respond positively to dog training school; after a quick look around, these dogs are ready to work!

More typically, dogs experience some degree of discomfort which may be expressed as mild anxiety. Anxiety is the mind's reaction when we aren't sure if we need to be afraid or not. If the anxiety is mild, and if nothing bad actually happens, then most typical dogs can move through this stage relatively quickly and relax at dog school.

But there are other dogs, just as with people, who do not adapt very well. They have more than mild anxiety: they feel fear. They are sure that they are in danger, and they respond with a typical fight, flight, or freeze reaction. Which reaction a dog expresses is a function of the dog's temperament, how the dog's expressions of fear have been handled in the past, and the extent to which she has a choice in the matter.

Dogs who react with fight will lunge towards the things that are upsetting them in an effort to increase the amount of distance between them. We call these dogs "reactive" because they overreact to the stimuli in their environment.

Dogs who react with flight will try to run away, also in an effort to increase the distance. If a leash prevents this option, then they often hide behind their owners. When a dog chooses flight but is pushed beyond her limits, she may then switch to a fight reaction in a last ditch effort to prevent perceived harm to herself.

Dogs who freeze do just that: they stop moving, or they move very slowly without showing any obvious reaction to what is happening around them. These dogs want to disappear, and they go to great lengths to make this happen. Freezing is also the classic response of dogs who have been severely corrected for showing either fight or flight reactions; they have learned that neither escape nor self defense will be tolerated by their owners. While a dog who freezes to avoid getting into trouble is no longer embarrassing her owner with her behavior, her emotional state of fear has not changed at all. Her brain has shut down, and she won't be able to respond to cues.

In all three cases, fear is driving the dog's behavior, regardless of its expression as a fight, flight, or freezing. And in all three cases, neither learning nor performing with any degree of focus or enthusiasm is possible.

So what does this mean for your attempts to generalize your dog's behavior to new environments? How will you work through your dog's distraction training?

You won't. You have bigger fish to fry.

Think about how you feel when you are frightened or when you think that your safety is at risk. I'm not referring to the nervousness you might feel in a new situation. I'm talking about that overwhelming feeling of dread that takes over and lasts until you believe that you are out of danger.

For example, if someone is trying to break into your house at night, what would you do? You might look for a weapon and come out screaming threats, whether or not you believe you could actually back those threats up. You might choose to run away by escaping out the back door and running to a trusted neighbor's house. Or you might freeze up, simply hoping this whole situation will go away.

Regardless of your personal approach to handling your fear, you are certainly not in a place to practice any skills that you may have recently acquired, no matter how much you may be motivated by those activities. You are not going to settle down and read a good book that you've been excited about all week. You are not going to sit down to a delicious meal that you prepared. You are certainly not going to study for an exam, chat with a friend, or play with your children. You can't. You're under the influence of fear, and fear trumps everything.

But what if the dog's fear is irrational? Can't that be communicated to the dog? Yes, it can... but that takes time. Remember that your dog is living in a human's world. If you were kidnapped by aliens and something waved its tentacles at you as you were approached by many other aliens, you would be as likely to believe that tentacle waving meant impending death as the possibility of new friends.

This dog's twisted leash, panting, and flattened ears tell the story. This dog is too nervous for the environment.

So what should you do when you discover that your dog is showing a fear reaction?

First, put aside your plans to train specific behaviors such as sit, down, or stay. Instead, focus on making your dog feel better, possibly with food, toys, or personal play with your dog. If your dog is feeling mild anxiety, but she is also experiencing positive things at the same time, then she is being conditioned to feel better in that environment.

You may be wondering about the wisdom of feeding, petting, or playing with a dog who is feeling fearful. Won't that reward the dog for being afraid? Simply put: no. You cannot reward fear because fear is not a choice - it's a feeling.

The dog on the left has his tail tucked and his ears flat. He is also ignoring his owner's offer of a cookie. He is not ready to work here.

Here's an example with a human (remember, learning theory applies to dogs and humans equally). If your child is experiencing mild stage fright and you give her some candy to eat while she waits, the candy will not increase her fear. Indeed, it is likely to reduce her fear because it both distracts her from her discomfort and also makes her associate the stage and the performing environment with something pleasant - eating candy. But if the child is so stressed that she cannot eat, candy won't help. You will have to hope that time and experience will help her work through her fear without your help. If she ends up enjoying her time on stage, then this is exactly what is likely to happen.

So how about your dog? If your dog will eat, go ahead and feed her something she enjoys with no strings attached. If you return to an area that makes your dog a little uncomfortable several times and you simply feed your dog while hanging out there, your dog should become more and more comfortable in that place. With time and experience, she will relax, and you can move forward with your training plans.

If your dog's fear level is very low and can be categorized as mild anxiety or simply hyper-excitement, then what I have described will work easily and quickly, and you can continue with the training laid out in this book.

It's okay to pick up a fearful dog!

But if your dog's fear is significantly greater - which may be indicated by heavy nervous panting, wet footprints on the floor, dilated pupils, and lunging at others - you need to stop what you're doing and move away. Your dog is too close to whatever is upsetting her. That is not mild anxiety; it is fear or panic. Overcoming fear using the process I have described only works if your dog is only mildly aware of her discomfort. Any outward displays such as lunging, trying to escape, or freezing means the dog is in over her head. It's time to leave.

Behavior work for deep anxiety or fear often requires professional assistance to be effective and safe. If you think your dog is expressing more than simple mild discomfort in new environments, put down this book and find a professional trainer who uses positive methods to help you work through these issues.

Reassure your nervous dog.

Chapter 16
The Habit of Cooperation

A habit is something that we do without much - if any - thought. We continue with our habits, even when they no longer make sense or we've long forgotten the reasons for our habit, because they bring us comfort.

Even small children can develop a cooperative relationship with a dog! Taz practices agility off leash and in public - willingly!

Dogs also form habits, and we can use these to our advantage. This entire book is about developing a habit - a habit of cooperation. We want our dogs to cooperate, over and over again in the presence of alternative options, even when we have nothing to offer in response or when what we have to offer is of a much lower value than the alternative that they are considering.

In addition, dogs are social creatures that value working closely and cooperatively with humans. Your dog WANTS to make the right choices and to cooperate, simply to get along in our human world. It makes them feel good! Once your dog understands what you want and how to get along, it is not likely that your dog is calculating the value of cooperation each time you request a behavior. Instead, your dog simply cooperates to earn less tangible rewards such as your personal approval, genuine praise and the occasional delicious morsel. But first they have to be trained to understand how to perform correctly, and that was the subject of this entire book.

When dogs cooperate, and when we are able to help our dogs develop this habit, we begin to see several positive effects.

The biggest one is that our dogs begin to respond to our cues without thinking about why they are cooperating. The cookies, praise, and generally positive atmosphere that result becomes a secondary expectation, but the primary response from the dog isn't even conscious; the dog cooperates because that is what he's been conditioned to do!

For the past few months, you have been working for about ten minutes a day to develop a habit of cooperation with your dog. And what has the result been?

Your dog has learned that positive things happen when he cooperates, but not every time. You've turned your dog into a gambler, and he knows that sometimes, cooperation will pay off. Not every time, but occasionally. You offer reinforcement just often enough that your gambler stays optimistic. Further, when especially difficult challenges are presented and your dog is successful, you make a point of providing a very special response. While a special response isn't always possible, often it is! The fact is, your fridge isn't that far away whenever your dog cooperates around the house. Keep that in mind.

Think about those performance dogs on TV. Those trainers have mastered the challenge of mutual cooperation and random reinforcement, and they have developed a relationship with their dogs based on cooperation. Those dogs know that they will not get anything in competition, but they work hard anyway, and they love doing it! They are working out of a love of interaction with their special human, for the value of the personal approval that they receive, and possibly most important, out of habit.

I hope this book has helped you develop that habit of cooperation and a basic understanding of the joy that comes with working with another species in a cooperative fashion. If you have worked through this book and found that you loved every minute of your training time with your dog, then read on to the next chapter. Maybe in your heart, you are a dog trainer. Not necessarily a professional dog trainer, but maybe you have the desire to find an even richer and deeper route to connection with your dog through competing in dog sports.

But even if you aren't interested in competition, you now have a dog you can take many places, confident that he will be welcome due to his good behavior. And ultimately, that's what dog training is all about: spending time with your dog - and enjoying it!

Gator loves to work even though he knows that he will not receive a cookie.

Dogs who are trained to cooperate even when they encounter distractions make wonderful companions!

Chapter 17
If You Want to do More...

About Competition Dog Sports!

If you purchased this book and took the time to work through the exercises in order to make your dog a more pleasant and reliable companion for you and your family, then you are not a typical dog owner. Only about 4% of dog owners seek out professional advice or read books on dog training when they acquire a dog, and far fewer go beyond one class on basic pet manners.

That means that by virtue of reading this book, you are different than the average pet owner. You want more than a dog sitting in your backyard, you want a true companion. You've shown a commitment to developing a deeper relationship with your dog. You look forward to your daily training sessions, and it appears your dog does too! You've discovered that as a result of additional training, your dog has become more attached to you and looks to you more readily for direction. In short, you've found that your soul feels richer when you're working together. What's available to you to continue on this journey that you've started?

Quite a lot, actually!

Competition dog sports are one of the most popular hobbies available around the world. The options are expanding every day for all different types and temperaments of dogs. Purebreds and mixed breeds, large dogs and small dogs, young dogs and old dogs - all are welcome in the world of dog performance sports. I have been training for and competing in competitive dog sports for more than 30 years, and those sports have shaped my life for the better.

Dog sports can bring tremendous joy to you and your companion when you train with respect. You'll discover more than just how smart your dog is; you'll learn how much your dog values her connection with you, in the same manner that you are learning to love your connection with her.

If you're interested in trying out dog sports, read on! This chapter will introduce you to some of the competition dog sports that are available to you. If you find one that piques your interest, you can learn more about the sport in a variety of ways. There are books aimed at dog sports competitors, local classes with private trainers or dog training clubs, and online training opportunities that can take you from the very beginning steps all the way to competition readiness.

Agility

Agility is a sport in which a handler directs a dog through an obstacle course in a race for both time and accuracy. Dogs run off leash with no food or toys as incentives, and the handler can touch neither dog nor obstacles. Consequently, the handler's controls are limited to voice, movement, and various body signals, requiring exceptional training of the animal and coordination of the handler. In competition, the handler must assess the course, decide on handling strategies, and direct the dog through the course with precision and speed equally important. Agility is probably the most popular dog sport worldwide, and with good reason. Dogs and handlers love it! Agility classes are easily found in most locations.

Raven competes in Agility.

Cooper loves tunnels!

149

Rally Obedience

Rally obedience (also known as Rally or Rally-O) is a dog sport based on obedience where the competitors proceed around a course of designated stations with the dog in heel position. Each station has a sign that instructs the team what to do, such as various heeling moves, calls to front, and jumps at the higher levels. Unlike traditional obedience, handlers are allowed to verbally interact with their dogs during the course.

Zen loves rally.

Nosework

Nosework was created to mimic professional detection dog tasks. One dog and one handler form a team. The dog must find a hidden target odor, often ignoring distractions such as food or toys, and alert the handler when she's found it. Nosework is a fast growing sport in part because it accommodates canines with disabilities or behavior problems. Nosework is highly amenable to online learning for those who can't find classes locally, or for dogs who struggle with fear or reactivity issues in a class setting.

This Aussie makes a find in Nosework!

Roxie enjoys scent games.

Flyball

Flyball is a relay race with teams of four dogs. The dogs race against each other over a series of low jumps to a spring-loaded box that releases a tennis ball when the dog hits it with his front paws. The dog must catch the ball and then run back to his handler with it. Each dog must return the ball all the way across the start line before the next dog crosses. Penalties are applied to teams if the ball is dropped or if the next relay dog is released early. The first team to have all four dogs cross the finish line wins the heat. It is a fast and intense sport!

Flyball is a high intensity, fast paced sport!

Chance is focused!

Tracking

Tracking encourages dogs to make use of their strongest faculty, their nose! The objective is for the dog to find the "lost" tracklayer and any articles that person may have dropped along the track. On the day of the trial, a tracklayer follows a designated path, leaving personal articles as specified by the judge. The track is then "aged" – or allowed to sit for a period of time – as determined by the organization and the level of competition. Then the dog and handler are directed to follow the track. In general, a dog must work continuously without assistance from the handler, and find the required number of lost articles to be awarded a passing score.

Winston enjoys tracking.

Urban tracking.

Competition Obedience

At an obedience trial, the dog and handler will perform various predefined obedience exercises, such as sit, down, stay, come, and heel. At the higher levels, jumping, scent work, retrieving, and following hand signals are included. The dog's performance is evaluated by a judge. A handler may choose to train for higher degrees of accuracy in order to receive more points. Obedience competition provides an opportunity for a person and dog to work as a highly tuned team.

The author competing in obedience with Raika.

Disc Dog

In disc dog competitions, dogs and their human partners compete to catch Frisbees. They may be judged based on the distance to which the disc is thrown and caught, or on the artistic merit of a routine in which dogs are encouraged to do spectacular tricks while performing their catches. Disc dog is an extremely popular spectator sport due to the wide variety of routines showcased by the different teams.

Disc Dog!

Soaring high in Freestyle Disc Dog!

Canine Freestyle (Dancing with Dogs)

Canine freestyle, also known as musical freestyle and dancing with dogs, is a modern dog sport that is a mixture of obedience moves and tricks which are performed to music. It allows for creative interaction between dogs and their owners. The sport has developed into competition forms in several countries around the world, and has become common in animal talent shows and specialty acts.

Cinnamon competes in Freestyle.

Astro is "King of the Road!"

Treibball

Treibball originated in Germany and entered sanctioned competition in the US in 2008. The dog must move large exercise balls into a soccer goal within a set time period, usually about 15 minutes. The handler must stay within a predetermined area. The dog works closely with the handler, who is only allowed to use whistles and verbal or hand signals to direct the dog. The dog and handler team are scored on cooperation and direction, and can earn extra points or accrue demerits accordingly.

Abbey competes in Treibball.

Acre drives the ball back to his mom!

Rally-FrEe

Rally-FrEe combines the trick behaviors from Canine Musical Freestyle with the station format of Rally Obedience. The dog may work on the left or right side, in front of, or behind the handler as they move through the course together. The sport emphasizes the precise execution of fundamental freestyle and obedience skills. "Free Choice" stations encourage the handler to teach their dog creative or complex tricks. Music is often a part of the competitions.

Kashi competes in Rally FrEe.

Finding a Local Class

Dog sports instructors vary wildly in their choice of training methods, so select your sport and trainers with care. Look for a class where the instructor is warm and friendly to both you and your dog, and where the dogs are wagging their tails and appear happy, engaged, and excited to be there! Look for the liberal use of motivators; if you see a roomful of unhappy dogs wearing pressure collars (prong collars, electronic collars, choke chains), decide if that is the relationship that you want to develop with your dog. If not, then move on.

Ask yourself, is this fun for me? Is this fun for the dog? Is this something that we will enjoy learning and practicing together? If not, look for another sport! You might have to investigate a few before you find the one that works best for you and your dog.

Do not underestimate the value of online learning. The Fenzi Dog Sports Academy is a large and well-respected online training school that specializes in competitive dog sports, with students ranging from absolute novices to highly sophisticated world competitors. At Fenzi Academy, you can be sure that you'll be receiving training that is kind to your dog, focused on having fun, and highly effective at preparing your team for any level of competition.

You can learn more at www.fenzidogsportsacademy.com

Thank you for taking time to read "Beyond the Back Yard! Train Your Dog to Listen Anytime, Anywhere!" If you enjoyed it, please consider telling your friends or posting a short review on Amazon, regardless of where you bought the book. Word of mouth is an author's best friend and much appreciated.

Notes

Notes

Notes